AMERICA the BEAUTIFUL

WYOMING

By Ann Heinrichs

Consultants

Emmett D. Chisum, Professor and Research Historian, American Heritage Center, University of Wyoming

Robert A. Campbell, Associate Professor, College of Education, University of Wyoming

Randy L. Adams, Historian, Teacher; Author of *Frontier Spirit: the Story of Wyoming*

Robert L. Hillerich, Ph.D., Bowling Green State University, Bowling Green, Ohio

CHILDRENS PRESS®

Skiers in Jackson

Project Editor: Joan Downing
Associate Editor: Shari Joffe
Design Director: Margrit Fiddle
Typesetting: Graphic Connections, Inc.
Engraving: Liberty Photoengraving

Library of Congress Cataloging-in-Publication Data

Heinrichs, Ann.
   America the beautiful. Wyoming / by Ann
Heinrichs.
     p.   cm.
   Includes index.
   Summary: Describes the geography, history,
people, and culture of Wyoming.
   ISBN 0-516-00496-4
   1. Wyoming—Juvenile literature.
[1. Wyoming] I. Title.
F761.3.H45   1991   91-544
978.7—dc20   CIP
                                           AC

P+b

Photographers at Yellowstone National Park

TABLE OF CONTENTS

Chapter 1
WELCOME TO WYOMING

WELCOME TO WYOMING

"Until woman's suffrage came among us, life was a drag—a monotonous sameness," wrote Laramie humorist Bill Nye in the 1880s. "Now it is not that way. . . . She purifies the political atmosphere and comes to the polls with her suffrage done up in a little wad . . . and redeems the country."

Life in Wyoming's early days was not really such a drag, as Nye put it. Fearless mountain men risked their lives opening up trails and passes through Wyoming's craggy wilds. Pioneers rumbled across the sage-dotted plains and through snowy mountain ranges, their wagon trains bound for the farmland and gold fields of the West. Next came cowboys, cattlemen, railroads, outlaws, and miners of gold, coal, uranium, and oil.

Yet Nye was right about the impact of Wyoming's women. They were the first women in the nation to vote, serve on juries, and hold public office. As they clutched their "little wad" of privileges, worldwide headlines blared the news, and Wyoming earned its nickname—the Equality State.

Unofficially, Wyoming is also called the Cowboy State. While women wielded their new liberties, cattlemen were kicking up dust on the range with cattle drives, roundups, and rodeos. To many, the bucking-horse emblem seen all over Wyoming signifies what one writer called "the purest cattle state of all."

Outsiders treasure Wyoming as a land of spectacular beauty. Yellowstone, the Tetons, Devils Tower, and Jackson Hole have enchanted visitors for centuries. In this land, with its natural splendor and precious minerals, is Wyoming's wealth today.

Chapter 2
THE LAND

THE LAND

Suppose a box were drawn on a map of the United States to enclose jagged mountains, treeless plains, red deserts, unearthly rock formations, dazzling waterfalls, spectacular gorges, spewing water jets, and eerie mineral springs. How big would that box have to be? The answer is, "Only as big as Wyoming," for all these features lie within Wyoming's borders.

Wyoming is one of the nation's western states. Besides Colorado, it is the only state whose borders are formed by four straight lines.

With a land area of 97,809 square miles (253,325 square kilometers), Wyoming ranks ninth in size among all the states. It is the fourth-largest of the Rocky Mountain states, a grouping that also includes Washington, Oregon, Idaho, Montana, Nevada, Utah, and Colorado. From north to south, Wyoming measures 275 miles (443 kilometers); the state is 362 miles (583 kilometers) wide from east to west.

Montana lies along Wyoming's entire northern border. To the east are South Dakota and Nebraska. Colorado and Utah border Wyoming on the south. On the west, the Equality State is bordered by Utah, Idaho, and a tiny piece of Montana.

TOPOGRAPHY

Two of North America's major land regions converge in Wyoming: the Rocky Mountains, in the western part of the state;

Red Canyon in the Wind River Range

and the Great Plains, in eastern Wyoming. Another large North
American land region, the Great Basin, covers a small portion of
southwestern Wyoming.

High mountain ranges make Wyoming's average elevation the
second-highest among the states, at 6,700 feet (2,042 meters).
Between ranges lie several high, treeless basins, or valleys.

The Continental Divide snakes its way through the Rockies
from northwest to south-central Wyoming. This chain of peaks
marks the dividing line between North America's westward-
flowing and eastward-flowing rivers. In southern Wyoming, the
Great Divide Basin interrupts the Continental Divide, which splits
and goes around the basin. Waters in the Great Divide Basin flow
neither east nor west, but remain within the basin. The Red Desert
covers much of this dry and dusty basin, where sagebrush and
some short grasses grow.

Wyoming's many mountain ranges include the Absarokas (left) and the Tetons (right), in the northwest; and the Medicine Bow Mountains (right on opposite page), in the southeast.

Both the Absaroka and the Bighorn mountains extend into northern Wyoming from Montana. These ranges join the Owl Creek and Bridger mountains to form a great loop around the Bighorn Basin. Between the Owl Creek and Bridger mountains, the Wind River has cut a scenic gorge called the Wind River Canyon.

The Wind River Mountains rise south of the Absarokas and extend southeastward like a long finger into central Wyoming. Part of this range, and the Wind River Basin north of it, lie within the Wind River Indian Reservation. Among the lofty peaks of the Wind River range is 13,804-foot (4,207-meter) Gannett Peak, the state's highest point. At the southern end of the range is South Pass, an important gap through the Rockies that was used by nineteenth-century travelers.

Yellowstone National Park, in the state's northwest corner, contains the most spectacular array of thermal (heat-produced) wonders in the world. These include hot-water geysers, such as the famous Old Faithful, and steaming, colorful mineral springs.

South of Yellowstone, the snowcapped peaks of the Teton range rise abruptly from the valley. Grand Teton, which rises 13,766 feet (4,195 meters), is Wyoming's second-highest peak. Jackson Hole, one of the largest valleys in the Rockies, is surrounded by the Teton range, the Mount Leidy Highlands, and the Gros Ventre and Hoback mountains. Other ranges in western Wyoming are the Snake River and Salt River ranges.

Extending into southern Wyoming from Colorado are the Laramie, Medicine Bow, and Sierra Madre mountain ranges. As they stretch deep into the central part of the state, the Laramie Mountains follow the arc of the North Platte River. A section of the Medicine Bow Mountains is called the Snowy Range. Here, above pine forests and sparkling streams, snow glistens from high

Eastern Wyoming is part of the Great Plains.

mountain peaks. The highest point in the range is 12,103-foot-
(3,689-meter-) high Medicine Bow Mountain.

In eastern Wyoming are the Great Plains. Sage and various
grasses cover these plains, where cattle and sheep have grazed for
more than a century. Few trees grow on the plains, except along
riverbanks. Irrigation has allowed this fertile but naturally dry
region to produce corn, sugar beets, beans, barley, hay, potatoes,
and other crops. In northeastern Wyoming, spilling over from
South Dakota, are the Black Hills. Here stands Devils Tower, a
stump-shaped butte rising 1,280 feet (390 meters) above the valley
floor.

Forty-three percent of Wyoming's land is privately owned. The
federal government owns 47 percent of the state's land area, and
the state and other public groups own the remaining 10 percent.

Cliffs of the Grand Canyon of the Yellowstone River

RIVERS AND LAKES

The waters of three of the nation's great river systems rise in Wyoming: the Missouri, the Colorado, and the Columbia. Their tributaries drain more than 90 percent of Wyoming's land. Waters of the Yellowstone River rise in northwestern Wyoming, eventually flowing into the Missouri and then the Mississippi River. Countless artists and photographers have tried to capture the beauty of the Grand Canyon of the Yellowstone and its upper and lower falls. On its way into the canyon, the Yellowstone's Lower Falls take a 308-foot (94-meter) plunge, almost twice the height of New York's Niagara Falls. Flowing north into the Yellowstone are the Clarks Fork, Bighorn, Tongue, and Powder

15

rivers. South of Thermopolis, the Bighorn's name changes to the Wind River, which has carved out Wind River Canyon. The Shoshone River, a branch of the Bighorn, has formed a deep canyon as well.

The Belle Fourche and Little Missouri rivers of northeastern Wyoming and the Cheyenne, White, and Niobrara rivers in the eastern part of the state also flow eastward into the Missouri. The North Platte River, a major tributary of the Missouri, drains the southeastern quarter of the state. Into the North Platte flow the Laramie, Medicine Bow, and Sweetwater rivers.

Rising on the west slope of the Continental Divide, the Green River is the major waterway in southwestern Wyoming. It is also the mighty Colorado River's major source. As the Green River flows south across the Utah border, it widens into Flaming Gorge Reservoir, lined with blazing red-and-orange cliffs and canyons. Henrys Fork, Blacks Fork, Big Sandy River, and Fontenelle and Horse creeks are some of the branches that feed the Green River.

In the western part of the state are several streams of the Columbia River system, such as the Snake River and its tributaries—the Salt, Hoback, and Greys rivers. The Grand Canyon of the Snake River cuts through the Teton, Snake, and Salt ranges before it leaves Wyoming for Idaho. Bear River, in the far southwest, flows into Utah's Great Salt Lake.

Most of Wyoming's natural lakes are cool mountain pools. The two largest are Yellowstone Lake in Yellowstone National Park and Jackson Lake in Grand Teton National Park. Among hundreds of others are Shoshone, Lewis, and Heart lakes in Yellowstone park and Fremont and Boulder lakes in the Wind River range. Flaming Gorge Reservoir and Bighorn Lake are the state's two largest artificial lakes. Flaming Gorge, shared with Utah, is backed up by Utah's Flaming Gorge Dam, while

The Snake River flows through Grand Teton National Park.

Montana's Yellowtail Dam on the Bighorn River forms Bighorn
Lake. Dams on rivers within Wyoming have created Pathfinder,
Alcova, Seminoe, Glendo, Guernsey, Keyhole, Buffalo Bill,
Grayrocks, and Boysen reservoirs.

PLANTS AND ANIMALS

Over the years, settlers drove away much of Wyoming's
wildlife. Some species dwindled; others have almost disappeared.
Still, many wild animals find natural homes in Wyoming's
national forests and other wilderness areas. One such animal is
the moose, the largest member of the deer family. The world's
largest elk herds live in northwestern Wyoming. Elk are also
called *wapiti*, a Shawnee Indian word meaning "white rump."

Bison (left) and pronghorn antelope (right) can be seen in the wild in Wyoming.

Thousands of elk spend the winter at the National Elk Refuge at the foot of the Grand Tetons. Rocky Mountain bighorn sheep, mountain goats, grizzly bears, and black bears also inhabit the mountainous northwest. Lynxes and mountain lions lurk there too, though they usually avoid human beings. Wyoming's grizzly bears may attack if provoked, and visitors are warned to leave them alone.

Millions of buffalo (bison), the largest North American mammal, once grazed across the Great Plains. A few small herds can be seen in Wyoming today. Motorists in Yellowstone park sometimes have to stop and let the huge beasts lumber across the road. Like grizzlies, buffalo are fascinating to watch but can be dangerous when irritated. Coyotes, mule deer, and pronghorn antelopes range through much of Wyoming's basin and high prairie land. Pronghorns, the fastest mammals in North America, can run as fast as 70 miles (113 kilometers) per hour.

Packs of wolves once roved through Grand Teton and Yellowstone national parks, but a wolf-killing campaign by settlers and government agents in the early 1900s wiped them out. In 1991, after a long debate, it was decided that wolves would be reintroduced into Yellowstone. Smaller creatures scurrying about the state include gophers, ground squirrels, prairie dogs, chipmunks, foxes, skunks, snowshoe hares, cottontails, and jackrabbits.

Trumpeter and whistler swans live around the wetlands of Yellowstone and Grand Teton parks, as do pelicans, great blue herons, rails, snipes, gulls, and ospreys. Soaring through the skies with their wide wingspans are hawks, falcons, golden eagles, and bald eagles, which usually nest near water. Wild turkeys, sage hens, pheasants, grouse, ducks, and geese are some of Wyoming's game birds. Juncoes, magpies, nuthatches, and chickadees are seen throughout the state. Several species of snakes slither through the forests and prairies, but the prairie rattlesnake is the only poisonous one. Wyoming's lakes, rivers, and streams are home to bass, grayling, catfish, pike, muskie, and several kinds of trout.

Wyoming's game and fish commission oversees the state's animal conservation efforts. Besides the National Elk Refuge, Wyoming has four national wildlife preserves. Federal laws protect some individual species, as well. With the lives of their sheep and lambs at stake, many of Wyoming's sheepherders resent laws that protect predators. Lambs are easy prey for eagles, for example, which by law may not be shot.

The types of plants that grow in Wyoming vary with the elevation. In the highest forestlands are the major commercial trees—Douglas firs, ponderosa and lodgepole pines, and Engelmann spruces—as well as mosses and lichens. Growing at lower elevations are mountain mahoganies and, lower still,

A band of elk browsing along the Madison River on a winter day

cottonwoods, aspens, willows, and hawthorns. Buttercups, goldenrod, evening stars, forget-me-nots, arnicas, and many other wildflowers brighten the mountainsides and high valleys. Clumps of sagebrush dot the plains, and greasewood, yuccas, and cacti grow where moisture is low. Many varieties of short grasses grow on the eastern plains, including bluegrass, buffalo grass, wheatgrass, redtops, and tufted fescue.

CLIMATE

Wyoming is generally cool, sunny, and dry. Though winters can be severe, the dry air eases the bite of frigid temperatures. Average summer and winter temperatures for the state as a whole would not reveal much about Wyoming's climate. Colder temperatures prevail in the mountainous northwest, where some areas register freezing temperatures all year round. Lower-lying areas have a more temperate climate. In July, for instance, the average temperature in the Yellowstone region is only 59 degrees Fahrenheit (15 degrees Celsius). Casper, on the other hand, has an average July temperature of 71 degrees Fahrenheit (22 degrees Celsius). In January, Yellowstone park averages a chilly 12 degrees Fahrenheit (minus 11 degrees Celsius), while Casper averages a more bearable 22 degrees Fahrenheit (minus 6 degrees Celsius).

Basin, in the Bighorn Basin, holds the record for Wyoming's hottest day. On August 8, 1983, the temperature there was recorded at 115 degrees Fahrenheit (46 degrees Celsius). The same temperature was recorded at Diversion Dam on July 15, 1988. The mercury plunged to minus 63 degrees Fahrenheit (minus 53 degrees Celsius) in Moran on February 9, 1933, setting the record for the state's lowest recorded temperature.

Precipitation—moisture such as rain and melted snow—averages about 14.5 inches (37 centimeters) a year statewide. Both rain and snow fall most heavily in the northwestern mountains and most lightly in the basins and plains. As little as 5 inches (13 centimeters) of rain a year may fall in parts of the Bighorn Basin, while the northwest receives 50 inches (127 centimeters). Only about 15 inches (38 centimeters) of snow per year falls in the Bighorn Basin, while the mountainous northwest is blanketed with about 260 inches (660 centimeters) of snow a year. The glistening snowcaps on some peaks never melt. High winds often sweep across the plains, where there is nothing to break their force. Gusting and swirling, these winds create blinding dust storms in the summer and snowy "ground blizzards" in the winter.

Chapter 3
THE PEOPLE

THE PEOPLE

Wyoming was one of the fastest-growing states in the country in the 1970s. Between 1970 and 1980, its population grew by more than 41 percent. By 1980, according to the United States census, there were 469,557 people living in Wyoming. Wyoming then ranked forty-ninth among the states in population, just above lowest-ranking Alaska. By 1985, the United States Census Bureau estimated that Wyoming had dropped to fiftieth place. Although Wyoming's population had grown to an estimated 509,000 by then, Alaska's population had grown larger still. The 1990 census confirmed Wyoming's fiftieth-place rank. With a 1990 population of 453,588, the state had even fewer residents than it had in 1980.

Casper and Cheyenne are the state's largest cities. Though Casper was long Wyoming's most-populous city, the 1990 census revealed that Cheyenne has surpassed it in size.

POPULATION DISTRIBUTION

Southern Wyoming, along Interstate 80 and the Union Pacific rail line, is the most heavily populated part of the state. About one-fourth of all Wyomingites live in cities and towns along these transportation routes. In fact, four of the state's seven largest cities lie on this strip: Cheyenne, Laramie, Rock Springs, and Green River.

About 63 percent of all Wyomingites live in urban areas, or cities and towns of twenty-five hundred or more people, while

37 percent live in rural regions. Most of the "cities" that appear on a Wyoming state map are small towns, widely scattered throughout the high plains and the mountains. It is not unusual to see road signs announcing a population of fifty, or twenty, or even ten.

If Wyomingites were evenly spread out across the state, they would barely be able to see each other. The state has an average of only five people for every square mile (two people per square kilometer), while the national average is sixty-seven people per square mile (twenty-six people per square kilometer).

WHO LIVES IN WYOMING?

About 98 percent of Wyoming's residents were born in the United States. Many are descended from Wyoming's early settlers, who occupied themselves with cattle ranching, sheepherding, or farming. Immigrants came to Wyoming from all over the world, too. Italians and Greeks came to work the mines and Basques came to herd sheep. Many Scandinavians worked in the logging industry. Sugar-beet farms drew Hispanics and German-Russians. Chinese, Irish, and many others helped build the Union Pacific Railroad and later worked as miners. After World War II, Wyoming's mineral industries attracted more newcomers into the state. A uranium boom in the 1970s and an energy boom in the 1970s and 1980s brought in record numbers of new residents seeking jobs in the uranium, oil, coal, and construction industries.

About 92 percent of the state's residents are white, compared to the national average of 83 percent. Hispanic Americans in Wyoming number about twenty-five thousand, making up about 5 percent of the state's total population. Some four thousand African Americans live in Wyoming, making up less than 1 percent of the state's total population.

Carnival stands at Cheyenne's Frontier Days celebration

Wyoming is home to about two thousand people of Asian descent. A great number of Chinese laborers came to the region to help build the Union Pacific Railroad in the 1860s. Later, many Chinese settled in southern Wyoming's mining communities. Wyoming is also home to people of Japanese, Vietnamese, and Korean descent.

WYOMING'S NATIVE AMERICANS

About seven thousand Native Americans (American Indians) live in Wyoming. They live throughout the state, although more than half live on the Wind River Indian Reservation. Eastern Shoshone and Northern Arapahoe Indians live on the 2.25 million-acre (0.9 million-hectare) reservation and own almost all the land. Energy companies that extract coal, oil, and natural gas from Indian lands are required to pay royalties to the tribes.

The Shoshone live in the north, west, and south-central parts of the reservation. Fort Washakie, Crowheart, and Wind River are their major settlements. The Arapahoe are concentrated in the southeast, with settlements at Ethete, Arapahoe, and St. Stephens.

POLITICS AND RELIGION

Since statehood, Wyomingites have elected about the same number of Democratic and Republican governors. In presidential elections, however, the state's voters have favored Republican candidates almost twice as often as Democrats. Lyndon B. Johnson is the only Democratic presidential candidate that Wyomingites have supported since 1950.

For most sessions since 1930, Republicans have outnumbered Democrats in Wyoming's state legislature, both in the senate and house of representatives. Residents of the larger urban areas of southern Wyoming tend to elect Democrats, while the rural population leans toward Republicans. Wyomingites have consistently sent Republicans to fill their two seats in the United States Senate and their one seat in the House of Representatives.

Protestant missionaries were among the first white people to travel into the Wyoming wilderness. The majority of Wyomingites who follow a religion today are Protestants, belonging to Methodist, Episcopalian, Presbyterian, Lutheran, Baptist, and other Protestant churches. Roman Catholics make up the largest single Christian group, however, comprising about 18 percent of the population. About 6 percent of Wyomingites are Mormons— members of the Church of Jesus Christ of Latter-day Saints. Jewish and Eastern Orthodox faiths also have small followings in Wyoming.

Chapter 4

THE BEGINNINGS

THE BEGINNINGS

PREHISTORIC WYOMING

For millions of years, the land that is now Wyoming was covered by a shallow sea. Gradually, dry land rose up and tropical plants and trees flourished in the warm, moist climate. Giant reptiles—dinosaurs such as the horned triceratops—roamed the swampy terrain. Mysteriously, the dinosaurs disappeared about 100 million years ago. Swamps gave way to low hills and grassy plains as the land grew ever cooler and drier. In this new climate, new species of animals appeared: crocodiles, miniature horses and camels, the rhinoceros-like Titanothere, and the piglike oreodont. Later, during what is known as the Ice Age, great rivers of ice, called glaciers, formed. The glaciers gouged out canyons, and their melting waters filled lakes and streams. Fossils of plants, fish, and other animals that lived over fifty million years ago have been found in the sediment of these ancient lakes and streams. Fossil Butte, in southwestern Wyoming, has yielded fossils of prehistoric perch, herring, paddlefish, garpike, stingrays, snails, and clams, as well as palm leaves and ferns.

WYOMING'S FIRST PEOPLE

People known as Paleo-Indians may have lived in Wyoming as early as twenty thousand years ago. Searching for new hunting and gathering grounds, these early people came from what is now Siberia. While the great glaciers were still melting, the people crossed land now covered by the Bering Sea into present-day Alaska. Gradually, over thousands of years, their descendents spread into the Rocky Mountain and the Great Plains regions to hunt giant mammoths, bison, and other animals.

Wyoming's Early Hunters used stone arrowheads and spear tips to hunt big game. Near Worland, scientists have found the earliest remains of these mighty hunters. Spear points and other tools from this site, along with piles of mammoth bones, are estimated to be over eleven thousand years old. Bison traps from this period have been found as well. The hunters herded bison into dry streambeds or sand traps. Unable to scramble out, the bison were then killed. Another method of hunting bison was to drive them over steep cliffs.

Throughout Wyoming are tools and weapons, some more than ten thousand years old, of the Folsom culture. Folsom people used spears with chipped-stone points to hunt bison on the North American plains. Stone hide-scrapers, bone needles, and other tools that have been found throughout Wyoming give us a glimpse into the Folsom people's way of life. Starting about nine thousand years ago, another group of early people lived for several thousand years in the Absaroka Mountains west of Cody. Because a thirteen-hundred-year-old mummy was found there, this site is known as Mummy Cave. In eastern Wyoming, meanwhile, other early people were mining quartzite for weapon points by digging great pits in the ground. South of Lusk, in Niobrara County, is one of a number of ancient quarry sites. Cowboys who discovered the site in the late 1800s named these pit mines the Spanish Diggings, believing Spaniards from Mexico had dug them.

A nineteenth-century drawing of Arapahoe and Cheyenne hunters chasing buffalo

EARLY INDIAN GROUPS

Various peoples migrated into Wyoming and out again, following the animal herds. Others gathered roots and berries, fished the mountain streams for trout, or hunted mountain sheep and smaller game.

Before the 1700s, ancestors of today's Shoshone Indians lived throughout much of Wyoming, while Crow Indians hunted in the Bighorn Mountains and the Bighorn, Powder, and Tongue river basins. Great herds of buffalo provided the Indians with meat, hides, and other necessities. Thousands of Indians used to converge at a Grand Encampment in south-central Wyoming to hunt buffalo and other wild game. In the 1700s, Cheyenne and Arapahoe Indians invaded the Crow and Shoshone hunting grounds. The Sioux, edged ever farther west by white settlers in the 1800s, in turn drove the Crow and Shoshone farther west.

Bannock, Blackfeet, and Ute Indians also migrated into
Wyoming from time to time. When white people first arrived,
there were about ten thousand Indians in what is now Wyoming.

EARLY EXPLORATIONS

It was not buffalo but beaver that lured the first white people
into Wyoming in the mid-1700s. Beaver hats were in high fashion
in Europe and America, and beaver furs commanded a high price.
Tracking beavers and other fur-bearing animals, French, British,
and American traders and trappers pushed ever deeper into the
North American wilderness.

François and Louis Joseph de la Vérendrye were probably the
first white people to enter Wyoming. Their father Pierre, a
French-Canadian fur trader, sent the brothers out to find a trading
route to the Pacific Ocean. It is difficult to tell from their journals
exactly where they went, but it seems they crossed northeast
Wyoming and sighted the Bighorn Mountains in January 1743
before turning back. Over half a century passed before white
people ventured into Wyoming again.

In 1805, François Antoine Larocque, a French-Canadian
working for Great Britain's North West fur-trading company,
traveled across northeastern Wyoming. Larocque wanted to see
how abundant the beavers really were and to persuade Indians to
trap for him. He followed the Powder River and Clear Creek,
crossed the Bighorn Mountains, and followed the Bighorn River
north into Montana.

Meanwhile, a new era of exploration of the American West had
begun. In 1803, the United States purchased from France the vast
Louisiana Territory, which spread westward from the Mississippi
River and included most of present-day Wyoming. The Louisiana

Purchase nearly doubled the size of the United States, and President Thomas Jefferson sent Meriwether Lewis and William Clark to explore the little-known Rocky Mountain region. Although the two never entered Wyoming, their explorations paved the way for those to come. As a guide and interpreter, Lewis and Clark brought with them a Shoshone woman named Sacajawea, who eventually settled among her people in Wyoming's Wind River Basin.

COLTER'S HELL

After Lewis and Clark returned with tales of abundant wildlife, trappers were quick to penetrate the new western lands. In 1807, Manuel Lisa of the Missouri Fur Company led a party of traders up the Missouri and Yellowstone rivers. At the juncture of the Yellowstone and the Bighorn rivers in present-day Montana, Lisa built a fort. With him was John Colter, a seasoned explorer who was accustomed to hunting in the wilderness, running from grizzly bears, and dealing with Indians. Lisa sent Colter out to make trade agreements with the Crow Indians of northern Wyoming.

Traveling on foot with a 30-pound (14-kilogram) pack and a gun, Colter spent the fall and winter of 1807-08 exploring Wyoming's rugged northwest. Colter followed the Stinkingwater (now Shoshone) River west of Cody, discovered Yellowstone and Jackson lakes, headed south into the Jackson Hole area, and eventually made his way back to Lisa's fort. Colter is credited with being the first white man to explore the Yellowstone and Grand Teton park regions.

Author Washington Irving later wrote of the Stinkingwater River's "gloomy terrors, its hidden fires, smoking pits, noxious

Jim Beckwourth (left) and Jim Bridger (right), two of Wyoming's finest mountain men

streams and the all-pervading smell of brimstone.'' He called the spot Colter's Hell, probably tracing his information back to Colter's own reports. Although later writers attached the name ''Colter's Hell'' to the bubbling, steaming Yellowstone park region, the frightful nickname originally belonged only to the Shoshone River west of Cody.

THE FUR TRAPPERS' ERA

In 1808, New York industrialist John Jacob Astor organized the American Fur Company to exploit the rich trapping grounds of the American Northwest. In 1811, he appointed Wilson Price Hunt to lead an expedition across the continent and establish a post on the Pacific coast at the mouth of the Columbia River. Hunt's party, known as the Overland Astorians, crossed northeastern Wyoming to the Bighorn Mountains, followed the Wind River south, and hiked to the Green River. They then crossed Jackson Hole and the Snake River and proceeded west through Teton Pass and on to Fort Astoria at the mouth of the Columbia.

Members of Astor's Pacific Fur Company, meanwhile, had reached Astoria by sailing around South America and up the Pacific coast. Hunt sent one of these men, Scot Robert Stuart, back to New York with messages for Astor. In 1812, Stuart's party crossed Wyoming, discovering South Pass along the way. A long-sought pass through that section of the Rockies, South Pass was to play an important role in Wyoming history throughout the nineteenth century.

Astoria was lost to the British in the War of 1812, and Britons soon became more active in the Rocky Mountain fur trade. In 1818, Donald Mackenzie of Britain's North West Company embarked on an expedition eastward from Idaho into Wyoming. Mackenzie came upon three towering peaks, which his French-Canadian trappers called the *Trois Tetons*. Mackenzie probably entered the Yellowstone region, as well. He brought back reports of "boiling fountains," saying that "one or two were so very hot as to boil meat."

William Henry Ashley and Andrew Henry of St. Louis organized the Rocky Mountain Fur Company in 1822. Among their recruits were men who would contribute much to Wyoming's exploration: Jim Bridger, Jedediah Smith, David Jackson, William Sublette, and others. Two black men in Ashley's company, Jim Beckwourth and Edward Rose, were expert trappers, guides, and scouts.

Jim Bridger, called the "Daniel Boone of the Rockies," was one of Wyoming's most colorful figures. After one long and winding trek through the wilderness, Bridger explained, ''I wasn't lost; I just didn't know where I was for a couple of weeks.'' An intrepid trailblazer and fur trapper, Bridger was one of the finest ''mountain men'' in the West.

In 1824, Jedediah Smith succeeded in leading a party west through South Pass and into the beaver-rich Green River Basin. From there, he headed north into the Jackson Hole and Yellowstone regions. Quite unexpectedly, Smith ran into Alexander Ross of Britain's Hudson's Bay Company, who was also trapping in the Yellowstone area.

THE GREEN RIVER RENDEZVOUS

Eventually, Ashley himself reached the Green River Basin. In the summer of 1825, he held the first annual Rocky Mountain fur trappers' rendezvous at Henrys Fork of the Green River. Somehow, year after year, Rocky Mountain trappers got wind of the date and location of this annual summertime gathering. Once assembled, they swapped tales and important geographical information, as well as such goods as furs, knives, and guns. Certain members brought supply caravans up from St. Louis every year.

During the rendezvous years, these daring mountain men penetrated deeply into Wyoming's unexplored wilderness and on into present-day Montana, Idaho, and Utah. They blazed trails, discovered mountain passes, mapped land and water routes, and learned about unfamiliar plants and animals. Trappers' journals reported encounters with Blackfeet, Sheepeater, Salish, and Nez Perce Indians. On an 1829 trek, William Sublette immortalized his young partner ''Davey'' Jackson by naming Jackson Lake and Jackson Hole after him.

A drawing of a trappers' summertime rendezvous

Although the Rocky Mountain Fur Company dominated the area, it was not the only trapping enterprise in the Rockies. "Free trappers," not working for any company, were welcomed at the annual rendezvous. However, trappers for the rival American Fur Company, who started showing up in 1830, were snubbed.

Another character on the scene was Captain Benjamin L. E. de Bonneville, a Frenchman in the American army. On leave in 1832, Bonneville led a wagon-train trading expedition along the North Platte and Sweetwater rivers and through South Pass. In the decades to come, thousands of wagon trains would follow Bonneville's route on their way to Oregon, Utah, and California.

In 1833, Bonneville and his party came upon a bubbling spring of oil in the Wind River Basin. The oil came in handy; the men used it to grease their wagon wheels and soothe their horses' boils. Bonneville had no idea that his discovery foreshadowed

Fort William, later called Fort Laramie, was founded on the North Platte River in southeastern Wyoming in 1834.

Wyoming's oil boom, almost a century away. By the time Bonneville reached Horse Creek of the Green River, his horses and mules were worn out. At that spot he built Fort Bonneville, which became one of the rendezvous sites.

In 1834, William Sublette and Robert Campbell established Fort William trading post on the North Platte River in southeastern Wyoming. Later renamed Fort Laramie, it was Wyoming's first permanent white settlement. The same year, Nathaniel Wyeth set up Fort Hall trading post on the Snake River in Idaho. At that summer's rendezvous, the Rocky Mountain Fur Company disbanded, making way for the American Fur Company.

MISSIONARIES TO THE ROCKIES

Occasionally, missionaries showed up at the rendezvous. One was Marcus Whitman, who removed an arrowhead from Jim

Bridger's back during the 1835 gathering. Asked if the wound had ever gotten infected, Bridger replied, "Meat don't spoil in the Rockies." Whitman went back east to recruit more missionaries, while his partner Samuel Parker stuck with the trappers.

On September 23, 1835, Parker preached the first Protestant sermon in Wyoming to a group of Salish Indians. Though mystified by the speech, the Indians left suddenly to go hunting when a herd of buffalo arrived. Marcus Whitman, missionary Henry H. Spaulding, and their wives appeared at the 1836 rendezvous. Narcissa Whitman and Eliza Spaulding were the first white women in Wyoming.

Jesuit missionary Pierre Jean De Smet attended the 1840 rendezvous on his way north to minister to the Salish. On July 5, just east of today's town of Daniel, he celebrated Wyoming's first Catholic Mass. De Smet later made excellent maps of the Rocky Mountain region.

THE END OF THE FUR-TRAPPING ERA

The rendezvous of 1840 — the last rendezvous — marked the end of an era. Several factors brought about the demise of the rendezvous tradition and the Rocky Mountain fur trade.

Such extensive trapping had thinned out the beaver population. At the same time, beaver hats were going out of style and silk hats were becoming the rage. Furthermore, Fort William and other trading posts gave trappers a more stable place to meet and stock up on supplies. Jim Bridger retired from trapping and built a cabin on the Blacks Fork River in 1842. Over the next year, the site evolved into a trading post known as Fort Bridger. It was a wise move for Bridger. He had built his post in the path of a great wave of westward migration that was just about to begin.

Chapter 5
WESTWARD TRAILS AND INDIAN WARS

WESTWARD TRAILS AND INDIAN WARS

At first, Wyoming's trading posts served the needs of trappers and mountain men. As trapping waned, the posts began to serve quite a different clientele—wagon trains. Beginning in the 1840s, various waves of emigrants from the East and the Midwest crossed Wyoming. On this arduous journey across rugged mountains and treeless plains, they stocked up on supplies at Fort William (later renamed Fort Laramie) and Fort Bridger.

For the 250-mile stretch across Wyoming, all the major westward emigrant trails came together to follow the same route. From different starting points, the pioneers converged at Fort Laramie, followed the North Platte and Sweetwater rivers, and crossed the Rockies at South Pass. Beyond South Pass, people fanned out along several trails, depending on whether they were heading toward the Pacific Northwest, California, or Utah.

WESTWARD HO!

Thomas J. Farnham was the first of many pioneers to strike out across Wyoming for the rich farmland of Oregon's Willamette Valley. He and his pack horses made the trip in 1839, and a group of about thirty people followed his tracks in 1841. The next year, Dr. Elijah White led a party of 112 people along what became known as the Oregon Trail. A thousand pioneer farmers packed their wagons and left Independence, Missouri, for Oregon in 1843, followed by another thousand in 1844, and three thousand in 1845.

Members of the Church of Jesus Christ of Latter-day Saints, also

A group of Mormon emigrants pausing at South Pass while on their way to Utah

known as Mormons, formed the next wave of pioneers. Driven from their homes in Nauvoo, Illinois, they headed west to escape religious persecution. Many people objected to the Mormons' practice of polygamy, the taking of several wives. In 1847, Mormon leader Brigham Young led a train of followers in ox-drawn wagons across Wyoming and into Utah along what was called the Mormon Trail.

In the years to come, thousands of Mormons made the trek by foot, pulling handcarts. Young encouraged Mormon converts from all over the world to "gather to" his settlement in Utah's Salt River valley and to spread throughout the West from there. By 1869, about eighty-five thousand Mormons had traveled the Mormon Trail.

The discovery of gold in California in 1848 unleashed a massive westward rush for gold. Again, Wyoming was the crossing ground. In 1850, tens of thousands of covered wagons followed the North Platte and Sweetwater rivers and threaded their bulky way through South Pass. From there, they crossed into Idaho and cut to the southwest, headed for California's gold fields.

As emigrants rumbled through Wyoming, they cut across Indian hunting grounds. Angered that the travelers were killing game, setting fires on the prairie, and spreading disease, Indians sometimes attacked the wagon trains. Sometimes, whites were caught in the middle as Indian groups warred among themselves.

Lieutenant John Charles Frémont was sent to survey Wyoming in 1842 and 1843. In his report to the United States Congress, Frémont stressed that the people traveling along the Oregon Trail needed protection from the Indians. In 1846, Congress agreed to build several forts along the trail and to send army troops to keep the peace. In 1849, the old trading post of Fort William became the important military post of Fort Laramie.

In 1851, the army called a great council at Fort Laramie. Delegates from several Indian tribes attended this large and colorful gathering, where the Treaty of Fort Laramie was drawn up. The Indians agreed to keep peace among themselves and to leave the whites alone. For its part, the United States promised to pay the Indians $50,000 worth of goods a year for fifty years. Later, when Congress reviewed the treaty, it refused to accept the $50,000 figure, and—without the Indians' knowledge—reduced it to $10,000. This was the first in a series of mistakes and misunderstandings by the government that fueled Indian hostilities in the late 1800s. In 1854, near Fort Laramie, the army's mishandling of an incident over a stolen cow escalated into what became known as the Grattan Massacre, in which Sioux Indians killed Lieutenant John Grattan and twenty-nine other men.

THE MORMON WAR

Meanwhile, from Canada to Mexico, Mormons had established hundreds of communities. In Wyoming, they settled in the Green River Valley, purchased Fort Bridger in 1853, and built Fort Supply nearby. As gold rushers saturated the West, conflicts often broke out between Mormons and non-Mormons. The federal government had problems with the Mormons, as well, because the Mormons were running Utah as a Mormon territory and tended to ignore the wishes of federal authorities.

In 1857, President James Buchanan sent army troops under Colonel Albert S. Johnson into Mormon territory. In the so-called Mormon War that followed, the Mormons fled southwest Wyoming, burning Fort Bridger and Fort Supply as they left. Johnson rebuilt Fort Bridger as a military fort in 1858, and the post continued to supply and protect westward-bound traffic. That traffic included both the stagecoach service known as the Overland Stage, and the Pony Express.

THE PONY EXPRESS

A fast-mail service between St. Joseph, Missouri, and Sacramento, California, the Pony Express charged $5.00 per half-ounce (14-gram) letter and $3.50 per ten-word telegram. Messages passed from rider to rider at relay stations along the route, and traveled an average speed of 250 miles (402 kilometers) a day.

Brash and daring, yet highly skilled, the Pony Express riders braved storms, deserts, and canyons, hostile Indians and vicious wolves, to carry out their task. Riders—who included "Buffalo Bill" Cody and "Wild Bill" Hickok—were given Bibles and were forbidden to drink or swear. This amazing relay system, begun in

April 1860, lasted only a year and a half. Cross-country telegraph lines, completed in 1861, carried news faster than the fleetest rider ever could. That year, the Pony Express, a wildly successful experiment, was retired.

POWDER RIVER BATTLES

When army troops were called from Wyoming to fight in the American Civil War (1861-65), intertribal Indian warfare flared up again. Then, in 1862, the discovery of gold in Montana unleashed a new gold rush, and wagon trains rattled through Wyoming along a new route. John M. Bozeman opened a trail from Colorado to Montana through Wyoming's Powder River Basin. This was prime hunting ground, and the Sioux, Arapahoe, and Cheyenne Indians let loose their fury. Jim Bridger's 1864 trail through the Bighorn Basin to Montana's gold fields was a much safer route, since it did not cross Indian territory. But there was not much water or grass along this trail, so only a few wagon trains used it.

The army sent men up the Bozeman Trail to scout out sites for a new set of protective forts. This Powder River Expedition was fraught with trouble. In the 1865 Battle of Tongue River near the Montana border, General Patrick Connor charged the Cheyenne and Arapahoe villages of Black Bear and Old Devil. A month later, near the same spot, Indians battled Colonel James Sawyer's expedition for thirteen days.

Trouble on the "Bloody Bozeman" led to another council at Fort Laramie in 1866. Yet, even as army and Indian delegates met, the army was building Fort Phil Kearny and other posts to guard the Bozeman Trail. Sioux chief Red Cloud promptly declared the council a sham and, fed up with the trespassing, went on the warpath. According to one officer, the Indians attacked "nearly every train and person that attempted to pass over the Montana Road." Not even a soldier was safe if he wandered very far from his fort. Red Cloud surrounded Fort Phil Kearny with warriors in what was known as the Circle of Death.

In December 1866, Lieutenant Colonel William J. Fetterman set out from Fort Phil Kearny with eighty-one men to rescue a besieged wood-cutting party from the post. On December 21, in what became known as the Fetterman Massacre, Red Cloud and Sioux chief Crazy Horse ambushed and killed the whole party. In the Wagon Box Fight of August 1867, a timber-cutting crew near Fort Phil Kearny fended off Sioux and Cheyenne warriors from behind their overturned wagons.

Red Cloud finally agreed to negotiate, and an agreement was worked out in the Fort Laramie Treaty of 1868. The Bozeman Trail, Fort Phil Kearny, and two other forts were closed. All land north of the North Platte River and east of the Bighorn Mountains was recognized as Indian territory, where no whites might intrude. Indians also agreed not to interfere with construction of the Union Pacific Railroad across southern Wyoming. In a separate treaty made at Fort Bridger, the Shoshone Indians under Chief Washakie were allotted a reservation in the Wind River Valley. A shaky peace resumed.

RAILROAD TOWNS

Meanwhile, railroad men's dreams of a transcontinental railroad were about to come true. Central Pacific crews were laying track eastward from California, while Union Pacific crews built westward from Nebraska. Cheyenne was the Union Pacific's first terminal in Wyoming. The town was born on July 4, 1867,

Railroads came to Wyoming in the 1860s, bringing a new wave of settlers.

and within months, Cheyenne's population numbered in the thousands. Laramie, the next station, grew up the same way. A group of outlaws practically ran Laramie until law-abiding citizens formed a vigilante posse and drove out the riffraff.

Both Rawlins and Evanston were born as railroad towns. The population of each new "farthest west" town skyrocketed as tracks drew near, then shrank when the tracks moved westward.

Railroad construction crews were large and well organized. Many Irish, Chinese, Scandinavian, and Hispanic immigrants were hired to help lay the tracks. The Chinese were often the victims of violent discrimination. Striking miners raided Rock Springs's Chinatown in 1885, killing thirty Chinese and burning every building in sight.

The Union Pacific hired buffalo hunters, too, to provide food for the crews. William Cody earned $500 a month, as well as the nickname "Buffalo Bill," by providing a construction camp with ten to twelve buffalos a day.

Left: Women voting in Wyoming Territory in the late 1800s
Right: Esther Hobart Morris, the nation's first female judge

By 1869, the tracks had moved on into Utah. On May 10, 1869, at Promontory, Utah, the "golden spike" was driven in, linking the Union Pacific and Central Pacific lines. At last, trains could run all the way from the Atlantic Ocean to the Pacific.

WYOMING TERRITORY AND WOMEN'S RIGHTS

As their numbers grew, Wyomingites began to clamor for official status as a United States territory. On July 25, 1868, the Wyoming Organic Act created the Territory of Wyoming out of parts of Idaho, Utah, and Dakota territories. President Ulysses S. Grant appointed Brigadier General John A. Campbell as territorial governor, Cheyenne was declared the territorial capital, and the first territorial legislature convened on October 12, 1869.

The new territory lost no time in taking a stand on the issue of women's rights. When William H. Bright introduced a woman-suffrage bill, some legislators thought it was a joke. Most, however, thought it was either an interesting experiment or a good advertisement to draw new settlers. On December 10, 1869, the territorial legislature passed the nation's first act granting women the right to vote and to hold public office.

Just two months later, Esther Hobart Morris was appointed as South Pass City's justice of the peace, becoming the nation's first female judge. She and another woman judge, a newspaper reported, were "the terror of all rogues, and afford infinite delight to all lovers of peace and virtue."

Jury duty was the next barrier broken by Wyoming women. In March 1870, reporters from all over the country flocked to Laramie's district court when the first women served on juries. Frustrated photographers were unable to capture the historic moment, however, because the women sat behind veils. Newspaper cartoonists drew women jurors bouncing squalling babies on their knees, with the typical caption reading: "Baby, Baby, don't get in a fury; Your mamma's gone to sit on the jury."

In the fall of 1870, seventy-year-old "Grandma" Eliza Swain cast her ballot at the Laramie polls, becoming the first woman in American history to vote in a general election. In 1894, Estelle Reel became the first woman in the nation to hold a state elective office when she was voted Wyoming's superintendent of education. Mary G. Bellamy became the first female state legislator in 1911. Wyoming women were to find that the door of equality swung both ways; Anna Richey was convicted and sentenced to jail for cattle rustling in 1919.

Not everyone in Wyoming was happy about the new rights granted to women. When women served on juries, male jurors were not allowed their usual practices of smoking, drinking, and chewing tobacco in court. Also, it seemed that women were quicker to convict defendants and imposed stiffer sentences. In 1871, the use of women on Wyoming juries was discontinued.

After that, except in rare cases, women in Wyoming were not summoned for jury duty until 1950.

THE LAST OF THE INDIAN WARS

A rumor of gold was all it took for whites to break their peace treaty with the Indians. In 1874, prospectors rushed into the Black Hills of northeastern Wyoming and western South Dakota. By the treaty of 1868, this region was clearly off limits to whites. The intrusions unleased the Indians' fury, and the army just as furiously set about squelching it.

In the Dull Knife Battle of November 1876, General Ranald MacKenzie attacked the winter camp of Northern Cheyenne chief Dull Knife on the Red Fork of the Powder River. Many Indians, their homes demolished, froze to death in the mountains. In despair, most of the Cheyenne chiefs surrendered. This was the last major battle of Wyoming's Indian wars. In 1877, the Arapahoe were settled on the Shoshone's Wind River reservation until the government could decide where to assign them, and there they remained.

BANDITS, CATS, AND THE DEADWOOD STAGE

In 1876, the stagecoach service known as the Cheyenne-Deadwood Stage began its run from Cheyenne to Deadwood, South Dakota, in the Black Hills gold fields. Bandits plagued the route, robbing passengers and stealing mail and cargoes of gold. Lawmen had their hands full trying to catch the outlaws. The stage continued its run for ten years.

Trains and stagecoaches were the outlaws' favorite prey. They knew there were never enough soldiers and lawmen to cover all

those trails. Outlaw "Big Nose" George Parrott liked to hide out near Sheridan whenever he robbed the Deadwood Stage. So did the infamous brothers Frank and Jesse James.

Southwest of Kaycee was another favorite hideout. Red Canyon, or Hole-in-the-Wall, sometimes sheltered Wyoming's most notorious gang, the "Wild Bunch," led by Butch Cassidy and Harry Longbaugh, better known as the Sundance Kid. Gang members left messages for each other in nooks in the canyon walls.

A shipment of cats was the strangest cargo ever transported on the Deadwood Stage. A freight hauler named Phatty Thompson figured he could make a good profit selling cats to Deadwood dance-hall girls. Thompson combed the streets of Cheyenne, paying children twenty-five cents apiece for cats. On the way to Deadwood, the coach overturned and Thompson's huge crate of meowing freight busted open. Thompson lured back most of the cats by dangling food in front of them. In Deadwood, the pets fetched prices as high as $25.00 apiece.

Chapter 6
THE WILD WEST MEETS
THE TWENTIETH CENTURY

THE WILD WEST MEETS
THE TWENTIETH CENTURY

In real life, "cowboys and Indians" led harsh, often brutal, lives. Almost single-handedly, William "Buffalo Bill" Cody gave them a thrilling, romantic image. Famous as a Pony Express rider, buffalo hunter, and army scout, Buffalo Bill was the featured hero in an 1869 dime novel. In 1872, he went on stage to play himself, gaining even more fame.

In 1883, Cody organized "Buffalo Bill's Wild West and Congress of Rough Riders of the World." This dramatic extravaganza thrilled audiences with buffalo herds, shooting and roping exhibitions, reenactments of famous battles, and Indians in full traditional dress. "Little Sure Shot" Annie Oakley was a regular performer, and Sioux chief Sitting Bull even joined the show for a season. The show's thirty-year tour included appearances at Queen Victoria's jubilee in London in 1887 and at the Chicago World's Fair in 1893.

Land developers in northwest Wyoming, figuring Cody was "probably the best advertised man in the world," invited him to head their venture. Thus began the town of Cody, where Buffalo Bill built the Irma Hotel, named for his youngest daughter.

THE REIGN OF THE CATTLE BARONS

The Texas Cattle Trail was yet another historic byway, this one running through eastern Wyoming. In the 1870s, cattlemen began driving great herds of Texas longhorn cattle through the Dakotas into Wyoming and Montana to graze on the wide-open range. In 1884 alone, some eight hundred thousand longhorns trotted up the trail. Wealthy Wyoming cattlemen had thousands of longhorns herded north to their own ranches. In Wyoming's open-range system, each rancher marked his cattle with his ranch's brand. Everyone's cattle then grazed freely on the range, where rustlers could easily steal cattle and change their brands. Anyone could claim an unbranded animal, or maverick.

In 1873, ranchers formed the Laramie County Stock Growers' Association, which eventually grew into the Wyoming Stock Growers' Association. Through this alliance, Wyoming's "cattle barons" came to wield great power over the land and the legislature. Laws were passed regulating roundup times and branding practices. Ranchers were required to register their brands, thereby making it harder for rustlers to get away with changing the marks. The Maverick Law of 1884 outlawed the taking of mavericks. Detectives were employed by the Wyoming Stock Growers' Association to patrol the open range for rustlers.

In the 1880s, the ranchers' list of enemies got longer and longer. Sheepmen were competing with cattlemen for grazing lands. After the bitter winter of 1886-87 killed off thousands of cattle, many ranchers went out of business, and unemployed cowboys joined the ranks of the rustlers. Moreover, new homesteading laws were bringing a new wave of settlers into Wyoming. The homesteaders began breaking up the old cattleman code of the open range. As they fenced off their parcels of land, they divided up the open range, often fencing in valuable streams and watering holes. Settlers were building up their own herds, too, by taking mavericks. Many of the cattle barons viewed the homesteaders as just a new sort of rustler.

To identify his cattle and guard against rustlers, each Wyoming rancher marked his cattle (left) with his ranch's distinctive brand (right).

STATEHOOD

Wyoming's population more than tripled during the 1880s, growing from 20,789 to 62,555. In 1888, the territorial legislature sent a petition for statehood to the United States Congress. The next year, delegates met for a constitutional convention in Cheyenne. They debated long and hard about county lines, water rights, judges' salaries—and women's voting rights. Some delegates were afraid that Congress would not approve their constitution if it allowed women to vote.

According to legend, "We won't come in without our women!" was a resounding cry in Wyoming, but no one can trace the statement. It could be a short version of delegate Charles Burritt's impassioned testimony: "If they will not let us in with this plank in our constitution, we will stay out forever." Women's rights stayed in, and Congress approved the constitution. On July 10,

Sheep being herded across the Platte River near Alcova in 1903

1890, President Benjamin Harrison signed a bill making Wyoming the forty-fourth state in the Union.

Back in Wyoming, people celebrated with bells, whistles, firecrackers, and cannons. Voters elected Francis E. Warren as their first governor, but he served for only a few months. Warren resigned to represent Wyoming in the United States Senate, and Amos Barber succeeded him as governor.

RANGE WARS

The new state still had old problems to solve, as the so-called Johnson County War proved. In 1892, small-scale cattlemen in Johnson County decided to hold an early roundup. Besides being against the law, this made for a hazy distinction between a rustler and a regular cattleman. After all, Johnson County was rife with rustlers, and its town of Buffalo had a reputation as the "rustlers' capital." Furious cattle kings hired a band of gunmen from Hardin County, Texas, and prepared a list of the so-called rustlers in Johnson County. These rustlers were to be wiped out by an armed force made up of both Wyoming cattlemen and the hired guns from Texas.

The Invaders, as this armed force was called, marched from Casper toward Buffalo with their "dead list" in hand. On the way, they shot two suspected rustlers at the KC Ranch. Settlers rushed into Buffalo, named themselves the Home Defenders, and armed themselves to the teeth. The Invaders never made it to Buffalo but instead surrendered to authorities. Though some of the Invaders were charged with murder, witnesses conveniently disappeared and the charges were dropped.

In the aftermath of the Johnson County War, cattlemen hired Tom Horn, a former Indian scout who had also worked for the Pinkerton Detective Agency, as a "range detective" to spy on rustlers. However, Horn's job soon became that of a professional killer. Cattlemen paid him to shoot small ranchers or any individual on the ranges engaged in branding a maverick. He collected his reward by placing a rock under the victim's head. Horn made a fatal mistake when, in 1901, he shot a thirteen-year-old boy named Willie Nickell. He confessed that cattlemen had paid him $500 to kill Willie's father, who was grazing his sheep on cattle land near Iron Mountain. He had mistaken the boy for the man. Horn was convicted and hanged.

The last of the great range wars took place in 1909 in the Bighorn Basin, where cattlemen and sheepmen were at war. Cattle ranchers hated sheep, claiming they nibbled the grass too short, trampled the ground, and dirtied the streams. Cattlemen shot sheepherders, dynamited flocks, or drove them over cliffs. Like other ranchers in the state, they established a line that sheepmen were not to cross. They called it the dead line, because whoever crossed it could expect to be killed. Sure enough, on Spring Creek near Ten Sleep, some sheepmen crossed the line. Masked cattlemen raided their camp by night, killed three men, and burned their bodies. This time, several of the raiders were convicted and sent to jail.

As the range problems settled down, Wyoming turned its attention to more positive business. The state's population continued to grow in the early 1900s, and so did Wyoming's tourism industry. Yellowstone had become the world's first national park by an act of Congress in 1872, and President Theodore Roosevelt declared Devils Tower the first national monument in 1906. Agriculture was thriving as new dams brought irrigation water to dry land. Pathfinder Dam on the North Platte River was completed in 1909; Shoshone Dam (now Buffalo Bill Dam) on the Shoshone River was finished in 1910.

In 1912, a great gusher of oil spewed forth in the Salt Creek Field north of Casper. Pipelines were laid and refineries were built in Casper, which became the center of the state's petroleum industry. More wells were drilled in other oil-rich fields. Hundreds of workers swarmed into the state seeking oil-industry jobs. With the oil royalties it collected, the state was able to build new roads and schools.

WORLD WAR I AND THE 1920s

When the United States entered World War I in 1917, a full 7 percent of Wyoming's population went off to war. Commanding the American forces against Germany was General John Joseph Pershing, who became army chief of staff in 1921. Pershing was a favorite of Wyomingites. While stationed in Cheyenne, he had met and married Frances Warren, daughter of senator and former governor Francis E. Warren. One of Cheyenne's main streets, Pershing Avenue, was eventually named in honor of the general.

A photograph from the 1920s of a souvenir shop at Yellowstone National Park

Tourism continued to thrive in the 1920s as brand-new automobiles crisscrossed Wyoming on brand-new state roads. Dozens of dude ranches opened up to meet the desire of Easterners to live like Westerners for a few days. Congress created Grand Teton National Park in 1929, attracting still more tourists to the area.

In 1924, Wyomingites elected Nellie Tayloe Ross governor. The nation's first woman governor, Nellie Ross went on to become the first woman director of the United States Mint.

TEAPOT DOME AND THE 1930s

The Teapot Dome scandal put Wyoming on the front page of just about every newspaper in the country. In 1922, United States Secretary of the Interior Albert B. Fall secretly leased the federally owned Teapot Dome oil reserve to Harry F. Sinclair's Mammoth Crude Oil Company. The reserve, just south of the Salt Creek

After World War II, Wyoming's economy became increasingly dependent on the production of such minerals as coal.

Field, was named for a rock formation that looks like a teapot.

Over the next five years, Mammoth drilled dozens of wells and extracted millions of barrels of oil. In 1927, after a government investigation, Sinclair had to give his entire operation back to the government. Albert Fall was fined $300,000 and sentenced to three years in jail.

In the 1930s, the Great Depression swept the nation as banks, businesses, and farms failed. Wyoming, however, kept up its oil production and its irrigation projects. The Kendrick Project, begun in 1935, was designed to bring irrigation and hydroelectric power to the North Platte River Valley. This three-part project included construction of Seminoe Dam, Alcova Dam, and the Casper Canal water distribution system.

In 1937, Shoshone Indians on the Wind River reservation sued the United States government over lands where the Arapahoe were living. Since 1868, Wind River had been a Shoshone reservation. The government had placed the Arapahoe there in 1878 as a supposedly temporary measure. Now the Shoshone wanted payment for the value of Arapahoe-occupied land and for the natural resources on it. The Shoshone won. They were awarded $4 million, and in turn, the Arapahoe claims were legalized.

WORLD WAR II AND POSTWAR GROWTH

Before World War II (1939-45), Wyoming's economy relied on mining, agriculture, and tourism. Wartime demand for munitions and other equipment encouraged the state's manufacturing industries. Wyoming made other contributions to the war as well. The state's cattle supplied beef for military rations, and its coal and oil provided fuels.

After the war, more valuable minerals were found beneath Wyoming's surface. Trona, a source of sodium carbonate, was discovered in the Green River Basin in 1947. Mining began, and Green River was soon known as the "Trona Capital of the World." New trona-processing plants were built near Green River in the 1960s. Uranium, an essential material in nuclear weapons, was discovered in the Powder River area in 1951. The federal government immediately became Wyoming's biggest uranium customer.

In 1960, Cheyenne's Francis E. Warren Air Force Base became the headquarters for the nation's first intercontinental ballistic missile squadron.

For decades, oil, utility, and railroad companies had been reaping huge profits from Wyoming's resources and taking those profits out of state. "Wyoming's Wealth for Wyoming's People" became a battle cry for politicians and citizens alike. In 1969, the state legislature passed a law requiring corporations to pay a high tax, called a severance tax, on minerals extracted from Wyoming. With new revenues from its coal, oil, gas, and other resources, Wyoming was able to pour much-needed money into its cities, school systems, and state highways.

THE ENERGY BOOM—AND BUST

In the 1970s, Wyoming's oil industry continued to grow, and coal production shot up dramatically. Coal-industry towns such as Gillette, Rock Springs, and Evanston became modern boomtowns. As people flocked to the state for mining and construction jobs, Wyoming's population grew more than 41 percent. With the boom, though, came all the problems of rapid growth: too many job hunters, not enough housing, inflated rents, and a grim array of social problems.

Wyoming's economy soon took a downward turn. After the boom of the 1970s came the bust of the 1980s. Uranium from other countries began to compete with Wyoming's ore. Also, international arms-limitation agreements slowed the demand for uranium. It was the oil industry, however, that crashed the hardest. When worldwide oil prices dropped in the mid-1980s, Wyoming's oil companies cut back on production. Thousands of Wyomingites lost their jobs, and thousands more left the state. By 1985, Wyoming's population had become the lowest in the country.

HORIZONS FOR THE TWENTY-FIRST CENTURY

As Wyomingites look forward to the twenty-first century, they face some critical challenges. The most urgent one is to diversify

Fires raged through Yellowstone National Park in the summer of 1988.

the state's economy. As one resident put it, "When oil is up, the state is up; when oil is down, the state is down." Wyoming's state government is working hard to attract new manufacturing industries into the state.

Meanwhile, Wyoming's agriculture and tourism industries are healthy. But they, too, have their problems. Environmentalists struggle with mining companies over whether to preserve land or utilize its resources. Out on the range, the survival of lambs and calves is pitted against the rights of such predators as coyotes. Wildfires raged through Yellowstone National Park in the summer of 1988. Though new vegetation is sprouting, the fires showed what a fragile resource Wyoming's wilderness can be.

Wyoming itself is in a fragile state, devastated by the energy crash of the 1980s. Yet, disasters have a way of flushing out surprising new developments. Like the new-flowering forest, Wyoming holds the promise of fresh growth in the years to come.

Chapter 7

GOVERNMENT AND THE ECONOMY

GOVERNMENT AND THE ECONOMY

Wyoming's first state constitution, drawn up in 1889, is still the law of the land. Since then, fifty-one constitutional amendments, or changes, have been added to it. At least two-thirds of the state legislators and half the state's voters must approve any amendment to the constitution. The same approval is required for the state to call a constitutional convention.

STATE GOVERNMENT

Like the federal government in Washington, D.C., Wyoming's state government is divided into three branches—legislative, executive, and judicial. The state legislature makes the state's laws. Like the United States Congress, it has two houses: a senate and a house of representatives. Voters elect the thirty state senators to four-year terms and the sixty-four state representatives to two-year terms. Wyoming's legislature meets every year. In odd-numbered years, it holds general sessions, beginning on the second Tuesday in January and meeting for up to forty workdays. Budget sessions are held in even-numbered years, convening on the fourth Tuesday in January and remaining in session as long as twenty workdays. If the governor vetoes a bill that the legislature has passed, the legislators can override that veto by a two-thirds vote in both houses.

The governor heads the executive branch of state government, which carries out state laws. Wyoming's governor, elected to a four-year term, may be re-elected any number of times. Voters also elect the secretary of state, auditor, superintendent of public instruction, and treasurer to four-year terms. The governor appoints the attorney general and the heads of the budget and personnel departments. Wyoming has no office of lieutenant governor, as do many other states. If there is a vacancy in the governorship, the secretary of state acts as governor until the next election.

The judicial branch of Wyoming's state government interprets laws and tries cases. The state supreme court, Wyoming's highest court, listens to appeals from lower courts. The five supreme court justices, appointed by the governor for eight-year terms, select one of their members to be chief justice. One or two judges, appointed for six-year terms, preside over each of Wyoming's nine district courts. District judges hear major civil and criminal cases, as well as appeals from lower courts. County courts, police courts, municipal courts, and justice-of-the-peace courts round out Wyoming's judicial system.

A county board of commissioners governs each of Wyoming's twenty-three counties. Each board is made up of three to five commissioners, who are elected to four-year terms. "Cities" in Wyoming are communities with a population of at least 4,000, while those with 150 to 4,000 residents are classified as "towns." A mayor and a city council govern most communities in the state.

EDUCATION

William Vaux opened Wyoming's first school in 1852 at Fort Laramie, where Vaux served as chaplain. In 1869, the territorial legislature voted to provide free public schools. Wyoming Territory's first high school opened in 1875. Today, about ninety-nine thousand students attend Wyoming's public elementary and

The University of Wyoming, in Laramie, was founded in 1886.

secondary schools. Others attend parochial schools, most of which are in Cheyenne and on the Wind River Indian Reservation.

Wyoming supports its public schools with property taxes and proceeds from state-owned land. Only a few states spend more on education per student than does Wyoming. The state superintendent of public instruction oversees the public school system, and the nine-member state board of education sets standards and policies for the schools.

By state law, children in Wyoming must attend school from the age of seven until they reach the age of sixteen, or complete eighth grade. The state's average educational level is 12.6 years of schooling. Seventy-five percent of Wyoming's adults are high-school graduates, whereas the national average is 67 percent. College graduates make up 17 percent of the adult population.

The University of Wyoming in Laramie, founded in 1886, is the state's only public university. Wyoming also supports community

An oil refinery in Cheyenne

colleges in Casper, Riverton, Torrington, Powell, Sheridan, Rock Springs, and Cheyenne.

STATE ECONOMY AND FINANCE

Mining is Wyoming's single most important industry. Production of petroleum, natural gas, coal, uranium, soda ash, and other minerals accounts for about 26 percent of the gross state product. The gross state product is the total value of all goods and services produced in the state every year. At the same time, less than 10 percent of the state's workers have mining jobs.

Various service industries generate about half the gross state product. Government is Wyoming's largest service industry. Local, state, and federal government operations produce about 18 percent of the gross state product. The government also employs almost one-fourth of Wyoming's labor force. Transportation, communication, and public utilities account for 12 percent of the state's product, wholesale and retail trade produce another 12 percent, and finance, insurance, and real estate generate about 8 percent. Construction, manufacturing, and agriculture together produce about 12 percent of the gross state product.

Individuals and businesses in Wyoming do not have to pay any state income taxes. Instead, the state government receives about half its revenues, or income, from property taxes, sales taxes, and taxes on mineral extraction. Federal programs and grants provide the rest of the state's revenues. Wyoming's natural resources are a significant source of state income. The state's mineral severance tax is the second-highest in the nation, after Montana's. Part of this tax money goes toward building highways, developing water resources, and helping local communities. The rest is held for the future in the Permanent Wyoming Mineral Trust Fund.

MINING AND MINERALS

Petroleum and natural gas are Wyoming's leading mineral products. About half of Wyoming's mining-industry workers are involved in extracting these two valuable fuels. After oil was discovered in the Salt Creek Field north of Casper in 1912, Casper grew to become the state's petroleum center. Much of Wyoming's oil and gas comes from a region called the Overthrust Belt, located in the southwestern part of the state. Stretching from Alaska to Mexico, this geological formation encloses great oil and gas reserves. Amoco and Marathon are Wyoming's largest oil production companies, while Exxon, Amoco, and Chevron are the major natural-gas producers.

Coal ranks second among Wyoming's mineral products. The Powder River Basin is by far Wyoming's richest coal-bearing region. The clean-burning, low-sulphur coal of the Gillette area is in high demand. Coal is also mined in the Green River and Hams Fork regions, the Hanna coal field, and the Wind River and Bighorn basins. Coal mining employs over one-fourth of the state's mineral workers.

Wyoming leads the country in production of trona, the source of a valuable industrial chemical. Ninety-five percent of the nation's trona comes from Wyoming. Trona ore contains soda ash, or sodium carbonate, used in glass manufacturing and other chemical processes. Green River is the center of Wyoming's trona mining and processing operations.

Uranium and bentonite are the state's other major minerals. Wyoming ranks second in the country in uranium production and in amount of uranium reserves yet to be mined. The richest reserves are in the Powder River, Shirley, and Wind River basins. Riverton is the state's uranium milling center. Bentonite clay, used in oil drilling, is mined in northeast and north-central Wyoming.

Gemstones found around the state include agates, jade, sapphires, rubies, and diamonds. Gold, copper, limestone, gypsum, zeolites, and building stone are some of the state's other valuable mining products.

AGRICULTURE

Scattered throughout Wyoming are about eighty-nine hundred ranches and farms. Wyoming's farms and ranches are huge—the second-largest in the country—averaging about 4,000 acres (1,619 hectares) each. Arizona is the only state whose ranches and farms are larger in average size.

Until the early twentieth century, cattle and sheep ranching were the mainstays of Wyoming's economy. Ranching still reigns,

Recently sheared sheep grazing on rangeland northeast of Cheyenne

second in importance only to mining. About 90 percent of
Wyoming's agricultural lands are used for grazing cattle and
sheep. Many ranchers lease grazing lands on the eastern plains
from the federal government.

Beef cattle and calves are Wyoming's most valuable agricultural
products. They account for almost two-thirds of the state's total
farm income. Wyoming ranks third in the nation in production of
sheep, lambs, and wool.

Only about 6 percent of the state's farmland is used for raising
crops. Still, Wyoming is among the top ten states in production of
sugar beets, dry beans, and barley. Hay is the state's most valuable
crop, followed by sugar beets, wheat, and barley. Other valuable
crops include corn, dry beans, oats, and potatoes. Wyoming farms
also produce dairy products, hogs, honey, poultry, eggs, and
horses. Goshen County, in the rich North Platte River Valley of

Hayfields near Jackson

eastern Wyoming, has more cropland than any other county in
the state. The Star Valley, on Wyoming's far western edge, is dairy
country, producing most of the state's milk, butter, and cheese.

MANUFACTURING

Most other states carry on more manufacturing than does
Wyoming. In fact, Wyoming has been called the least
industrialized state in the nation. Nevertheless, Wyoming's
factories and processing plants add about $408-million worth of
value to the raw materials they process every year. That figure is
called the state's *value added by manufacture*.

Wyoming's major manufacturing activities center around its
minerals. A number of plants process petroleum, coal, iron ore,
copper, and aluminum. Sodium carbonate is processed from trona

A farmer harvesting alfalfa near Worland

in the Green River Basin. Chemical plants manufacture fertilizers and other farm chemicals.

Factories in Wyoming produce a variety of nonelectrical machinery. This includes farm equipment, construction and oilfield equipment, and aeronautics equipment.

Many of Wyoming's farm products are processed into other forms. Refineries in Lovell, Torrington, and Worland process sugar beets into beet sugar. Other food-processing plants turn out meat products, flour, cheese, and cattle feed. Clothing, printed materials, cement, stone and clay products, and glass products are some of Wyoming's other valuable manufactured items.

FORESTRY

Forests cover about one-sixth of Wyoming's land area. Almost half the state's forestland is used for commercial logging operations. About three-fourths of Wyoming's commercial forestland is under the control of the federal government, the state's largest single landowner. Wyoming's principal commercial trees are Douglas firs, ponderosa and lodgepole pines, and Englemann spruces. Aspens and yellow pines also have commercial value. The logs are cut into boards at a number of sawmills in the state, while other plants produce pulp, plywood, and other wood products.

TRANSPORTATION

In the mid-1800s, Wyoming was a crossing ground for thousands of westbound wagon trains. After the Union Pacific Railroad was completed through Wyoming in 1869, trains replaced wagons for traveling comfort and speed. Today, motorists tour Wyoming on about 39,500 miles (63,567 kilometers) of roads. Interstate 80 is the state's major east-west highway, crossing southern Wyoming along the Union Pacific's route. For north-south travelers, Interstate 25 enters southeastern Wyoming from Colorado and runs through Cheyenne and Casper to Buffalo. There it meets Interstate 90, which runs east-west from the South Dakota border to Buffalo before heading north into Montana. Throughout the state there are excellent U.S. and state highways that snake through mountain ranges and reach remote areas.

Freight and passenger trains in Wyoming now operate on about 2,400 miles (3,862 kilometers) of track. Besides the Union Pacific Railroad, the Burlington Northern and the Chicago and Northwestern railroads serve the state. Three major commercial airlines provide service to Cheyenne and Casper, whose airports are the busiest in the state. There are about ninety other airfields throughout Wyoming, many of them serving small, private planes in remote areas.

Jackson Hole Airport is one of about ninety airfields in Wyoming.

COMMUNICATION

Wyoming's first newspaper, the *Daily Telegraph*, first appeared at Fort Bridger in 1863. Of the forty-five newspapers published in Wyoming today, ten are daily papers. Casper's *Star Tribune* and Cheyenne's *Wyoming State Tribune* and *Wyoming Eagle* have the largest circulations.

Wyoming's first radio station, Casper's KDFN (now KTWO), went on the air in 1930. KFBC-TV was the state's first television station, beginning broadcasts from Cheyenne in 1954. Casper's KTWO-TV has long been an aggressive force in forming Wyomingites' opinions on matters of public concern. Today, about sixty AM and FM radio stations and eight television stations broadcast in Wyoming.

Chapter 8
CULTURE AND RECREATION

CULTURE AND RECREATION

WYOMING'S SPIRIT IN ART

After the Lewis and Clark Expedition, "explorer artists" traveled with exploring parties to Wyoming and other western regions. While not all of them reached Wyoming, their art reveals the rich Indian culture, wildlife, and scenic landscapes of the western mountains and plains. One such artist was George Catlin, who traveled in the West from 1832 to 1839 making portraits of Indians. From 1832 to 1834, Swiss artist Karl Bodmer traveled the American West with German prince Maximilian zu Wied, producing many works of the American frontier.

Nineteenth-century artists from the eastern United States and Europe who painted scenes of the Rockies were part of what was called the Rocky Mountain School. The first artist to enter Wyoming and paint its scenery was Alfred Jacob Miller, in 1837. Soon after, the beauty of Yellowstone inspired German-born artist Albert Bierstadt to paint grand, almost mystical vistas of that region. In the 1870s, Thomas Moran was sent to the Yellowstone area with the Hayden surveying party. There he made sketches of the scenery in the Yellowstone and Grand Teton regions and later developed them into paintings. William H. Jackson was a photographer for both the Union Pacific Railroad and the Hayden party. The state commissioned him to photograph Wyoming scenery in 1892. A few decades later, photographer Ansel Adams,

Greeting the Trappers, **by Alfred Jacob Miller, depicts the excitement surrounding the start of a trappers' rendezvous.**

one of the foremost photographers of the twentieth century, captured Wyoming's grandeur in his dramatic black-and-white photographs.

Frederic Remington was one of many artists who came west on the new railroads. Remington celebrated the spirit of the West in his sculptures, paintings, and drawings. Dynamic works by Remington and other sculptors can be seen throughout the state. *The Spirit of Wyoming,* a cowboy on bronco-back by Utah sculptor Ed Fraughton, stands between the capitol and the Herschler Building in Cheyenne. Richard Greeves' sculpture *The Unknown* stands in the Buffalo Bill Historical Center's Braun Garden. Harry Jackson's sculpture of Sacajawea stands on the grounds of Riverton's Central Wyoming College. *The Family,* a sculpture by Robert Russin, stands on the University of Wyoming campus.

Cove in Yellowstone Park, **by Frank Tenney Johnson**

Frank Tenney Johnson's paintings and drawings of western subjects were inspired by his years at the Rimrock Ranch, a dude ranch west of Cody. Among the many other artists who captured Wyoming's history and spirit in their work are J. H. Twachtman, George De Forest Brush, John Mix Stanley, William Jacob Hays, and Allen T. True.

ART GALLERIES, MUSEUMS, AND FESTIVALS

Today, paintings by Wyoming and regional artists can be seen in museums and galleries throughout the state. Many hang in the state capitol in Cheyenne, the University of Wyoming's art museum in Laramie, Nicolaysen Art Museum in Casper, and the art gallery at the Wyoming State Museum. The Whitney Gallery of Western Art in Cody, part of the Buffalo Bill Historical Center,

Traditional Native American crafts, including beautiful beadwork, can be seen at the Wind River Indian Reservation in west-central Wyoming.

features a magnificent collection of western art. The Cheyenne Frontier Days Old West Museum in Cheyenne and the Bradford Brinton Memorial Museum in Big Horn also feature western art. Jackson's Wildlife of the American West Art Gallery is considered the best wildlife art collection in the world.

The Wyoming State Museum displays a wide variety of Plains Indian arts and crafts. These include wood carvings, hide paintings, quillwork, featherwork, beadwork, ribbonwork, and cloth applique. Weapons, tools, costumes, and other materials used by the Sioux, Shoshone, Cheyenne, Crow, Arapahoe, and Blackfeet are on display at the Plains Indian Museum at the Buffalo Bill Historical Center. Native American art is featured at the Mid West Gallery on the Wind River Indian Reservation at Fort Washakie. Galleries and museums in Riverton and Lander also feature Indian art. Beadwork and other crafts can be seen at the Indian Arts Museum at the Colter Bay visitors' center in Grand Teton National Park.

Every fall, at the Jackson Hole Arts Festival, artists show their work and give art lectures and demonstrations. The festival also features winners of the annual Arts for the Parks competition. Western artists from all over the country display their works at the Governor's Invitational Western Art Show and Sale in Cheyenne. This annual show takes place at the same time as the Cheyenne Frontier Days festival.

PERFORMING ARTS

The Cheyenne Symphony Orchestra and the Casper Civic Symphony Orchestra offer regular concert seasons. The University of Wyoming's music department presents performances by its orchestra, string quartet, and chorus. In the university's concert hall is a Walcker pipe organ, one of the largest tracker organs in the country. Some of the world's outstanding orchestras and concert artists include Wyoming cities on their tours. Many concerts and other performing-arts events take to the stage in Casper's new Events Center.

The Wyoming Summer Music Festival brings classical concerts and other musical events to Laramie, Cheyenne, and Saratoga. Headlining the festival are concerts by Wyoming's Western Arts Trio. The annual Grand Teton Music Festival in Jackson Hole lasts through July and August, bringing world-renowned musicians to its indoor and outdoor stages. Some of the featured orchestras, chamber ensembles, and soloists also perform in Cody, Thermopolis, and Sheridan, and conduct workshops and seminars.

Ethnic and folk music flourishes in many forms throughout the state. Rock Springs and Sheridan feature summer polka festivals.

Grand Teton National Park is a hikers' paradise.

Bluegrass festivals take place at Curt Gowdy State Park outside of Cheyenne, at Fort Bridger, and in Gillette and Sheridan. Near Buffalo, there is an annual Basque festival. Cody sponsors the Yellowstone Jazz Festival every July, and Riverton holds a Cowboy Music and Poetry Festival.

Casper, Cody, Sheridan, Lander, and Cheyenne all support community theater groups. Cheyenne's Little Theater performs in the vintage Atlas Theatre. Cheyenne, Cody, Jackson, and other cities offer hilarious entertainment with their summer melodramas. Cheyenne, Riverton, and Evanston all have children's theaters.

OUTDOOR RECREATION

Wyoming's many wilderness areas are ideal for backpacking, hiking, horseback riding, fishing, hunting, and camping. There are

White-water rafters on the Shoshone River

hundreds of miles of designated hiking trails in Wyoming. Some
of the more popular areas are the Absaroka Mountains, Bridger-
Teton National Forest, the Wind River Mountains, and Medicine
Bow National Forest. Adventuresome spirits also enjoy float trips
on canoes and rafts on the Shoshone, Snake, and Salt rivers and in
Grand Teton National Park. Since pioneer days, people have been
taking healthful swims in the natural hot springs of Thermopolis,
Saratoga, and Jackson Hole.

Snowmobiling and cross-country skiing are favorite wintertime
sports in Wyoming. From Jackson, people can take snowmobile
tours through the Jackson Hole area or sleigh rides to
Yellowstone. Snowmobile races and dogsled races are exciting
spectator sports. Cutters, or horse-drawn sleighs, race every
winter in Afton, Big Piney, Jackson, and Pinedale. In February, the
All American Cutter Race Finals are held in Thayne.

In the Jackson Hole area, downhill skiers enjoy Rendezvous

Peak, which rises above Teton Village; and Snow King Mountain, just a few blocks from the center of town. In the summer, people can ride Snow King's lift for a view of the surrounding valley. Grand Targhee, west of Jackson on the west slope of the Tetons, is another popular ski resort.

Trout fishermen know Wyoming for its thousands of miles of cold, clear trout streams and its clear mountain lakes. Many species of trout are found in Wyoming, including rainbow, cutthroat, golden, brook, German brown, and mackinaw. Among the state's warm-water fish are largemouth and smallmouth bass, crappie, walleye, yellow perch, and channel catfish.

Walkers embark on a sport enjoyed around the world as they take *volksmarches*—"people walks"—over designated trails in the state. Volksmarchers enjoy scenery and wildlife on brisk, 10-kilometer (6-mile) walks through Wyoming's state parks and historic sites. Hot-air ballooning is another popular sport. Every summer, Riverton holds a summer Hot Air Balloon Rally. In Rock Springs is the annual Desert Balloon Extravaganza.

Vacationers can get a taste of ranch life on Wyoming's dude ranches. Eaton Ranch, opened near Sheridan in 1904, claims the title of world's first dude ranch. There are hundreds of dude ranches throughout the state, many of them in the Jackson area, the Wind River Mountains, and the Bighorn Basin. Some are luxurious, while others are rustic, reached only by airstrip or dirt road. On the working ranches, guests help with various ranch chores, often including roundups and cattle drives.

FESTIVALS AND CELEBRATIONS

The ten-day Cheyenne Frontier Days celebration, held in the last week of July, has been an annual tradition since 1897. Besides a nationally famous rodeo, the festivities include Indian dances and other exhibitions. Rodeos are held all over the state. Cody, claiming to be the Rodeo Capital of the World, presents the Cody Nite Rodeo every night during June, July, and August. The Cody Stampede is a special rodeo held in July. Lander holds an annual Pioneer Days Rodeo and Parade, and Casper hosts the Central Wyoming Fair and Rodeo. There are rodeos every year in Buffalo, Dubois, Pinedale, Sheridan, Rawlins, and other cities.

Powwows are held every year in the Shoshone towns of Fort Washakie and Crowheart and in the Arapahoe settlements of Ethete and Arapahoe. The Shoshone and Arapahoe also hold sun dances every summer in several towns on the reservation. Every August, the Gift of the Waters Indian pageant is presented in Thermopolis's Hot Springs State Park.

Many festivals in Wyoming celebrate frontier lifestyles, such as the Buffalo Bill Historical Center Frontier Festival in Cody and Caspar Collins Days in Casper. The annual Green River Rendezvous in Pinedale recalls Wyoming's fur-rendezvous days. All summer long, South Pass City's Western Heritage Festival features living history demonstrations. Fort Bridger State Historic Site celebrates its days as a trading post and military fort with the annual Fort Bridger Rendezvous. Events include contests for shooting, knife- and tomahawk-throwing, firebuilding, and rattlesnake-wrestling. Worland's Oktoberfest and Buffalo's Basque Festival feature ethnic food, music, dance, and culture.

WYOMING'S STATEHOOD CENTENNIAL

The year 1990 marked the one-hundredth anniversary of Wyoming's statehood. In celebration, Wyomingites from one end of the state to the other recalled their frontier roots in special

Above: A calf-roping event at a rodeo in Sheridan
Right: Military veterans being honored at the Ethete
Powwow on the Wind River Indian Reservation

ways. The arrival of the telegram bearing the news of Wyoming's statehood was reenacted in Cheyenne. Citizens turned out for costume parades, frontier-days exhibitions, and memorials of all kinds. The Buffalo Bill Historical Center in Cody featured a special show, "Rendezvous to Roundup: The First 100 Years of Art in Wyoming." In Laramie, the restored Wyoming Territorial Prison held its grand opening.

From Casper to Cody, crowds lined the streets when the Wyoming Centennial Wagon Train came through town. On this month-long journey, dozens of covered wagons, hundreds of horseback riders, and a few one-horse buggies wound through dusty hills and plains. Camping by night and rambling by day, they followed the route of the Bridger Trail for 260 miles (418 kilometers) through the heart of Wyoming.

Chapter 9
A TOUR OF WYOMING

A TOUR OF WYOMING

ALONG THE UNION PACIFIC ROUTE

Cheyenne, the state capital, was Wyoming's first station on the Union Pacific route. Within the downtown area are several fascinating sites. The golden-domed, Corinthian-style state capitol building, first occupied in 1888, is roughly modeled after the nation's capitol building in Washington, D.C. A statue of Esther Hobart Morris, Wyoming's first female judge, stands before the main entrance. Other monuments and statues grace the manicured grounds. The capitol's three-tiered interior is a showcase of masterful woodwork, sculpture and mural displays, and stained-glass artistry.

A short walk from the capitol is the Barrett Building. Inside are the Wyoming State Museum and Art Gallery and the Wyoming State Historical Society. Visitors to the museum see thousands of items on display, including Plains Indians' clothing and handmade goods, Wyoming pioneers' home furnishings, objects from the USS *Wyoming*, and trappers' and cowboys' gear. The art gallery, within the museum, exhibits the work of local and regional artists. Not far from the museum is the Historic Governors' Mansion. From 1905 to 1976, this was home to Wyoming's governors, including Nellie Tayloe Ross.

The Cheyenne Frontier Days Old West Museum is one of the finest historical museums in the Rocky Mountain region. The

museum's world-famous collection of 126 carriages includes a
Cheyenne-to-Deadwood stagecoach, a popcorn wagon, an
ambulance coach, and a hearse.

Other attractions in Cheyenne are the Atlas Theatre, a national
historic site; the National First Day Cover Museum, displaying
rare and first-edition stamps; and the Romanesque-style Union
Pacific Depot, with its lighted clock tower. The massive hulk of
"Big Boy," the world's largest steam locomotive, is in Holliday
Park. F. E. Warren Air Force Base, once a cavalry post called Fort
D. A. Russell, is also a national historic landmark. Its museum
traces the site's military history.

THE LARAMIE AREA

Interstate 80 leads from Cheyenne to Laramie, but a nice
alternate is State Highway 210, called Happy Jack Road. This

Lake Marie is nestled in the Snowy Range of the Medicine Bow Mountains.

scenic route through the mountains passes Curt Gowdy State Park, named for the Wyoming-born sportscaster. It also offers access to the bronze Abraham Lincoln statue built atop Sherman Hill, the highest point on the route known as the Lincoln Highway.

Laramie was born in 1868, when the Union Pacific tracks arrived. Within three months, five thousand people lived there. Now Wyoming's third-largest city, Laramie is the home of the University of Wyoming (UW), founded there in 1886. It would take several days to see all of UW's museums. In the Art Museum are more than five thousand paintings, sculptures, and other American, European, and Asian artworks. Among the Geological

Museum's rocks, minerals, and fossils is a brontosaurus skeleton discovered in Sheepcreek. The Anthropology Museum traces human cultures in Wyoming from the Paleo-Indians to historic times. The university also has an insect museum, a planetarium, and a western-history research center. On Jelm Mountain southwest of town is UW's Infrared Observatory.

Wildlife and the environment are major themes at the Wyoming Children's Museum and Wyoming Children's Nature Center, which offer exhibits and hands-on activities. The Edward Ivinson Mansion, built in 1892 as a private residence, later became a girls' school. Now it houses the Laramie Plains Museum, with its valuable collection of items used by pioneer families of the Laramie plains area. In the museum's Children's Room are handmade toys from pioneer times.

West of Laramie is the Wyoming Territorial Prison, where Butch Cassidy and other outlaws spent some time. Owen Wister immortalized Medicine Bow, northwest of Laramie, in his novel *The Virginian*.

Two scenic highways run west of Laramie through the Medicine Bow Mountains, locally called the Snowy Range: State Highway 230, running down into Colorado and back into Wyoming, and State Highway 130, a picturesque route past snow-covered peaks and mountain lakes. Medicine Bow National Forest covers most of the Medicine Bow range. Here, Indians once gathered to fashion bows from the forest's mountain mahoganies and to conduct ceremonies to cure their ills. Both scenic highways lead to the lush Saratoga Valley, between the Medicine Bow and Sierra Madre mountains. Saratoga is a resort area known for its hot mineral springs. To the south is Encampment, once a copper-mining boomtown and, before that, a great campground for Indians on buffalo hunts.

AROUND THE GREAT DIVIDE BASIN

Rawlins, on the eastern edge of the Great Divide Basin, has been an important railroad town and livestock center since its beginnings in 1868. Rawlins's Old Frontier Prison became Wyoming's state penitentiary in 1901. Horse thieves, cattle rustlers, train robbers, and other criminals served time there until it closed in 1981. Coal, uranium, oil, and gas now contribute to the area's economy. Northeast of Rawlins, sand dunes and sagebrush surround Seminoe Lake, the trout-filled centerpiece of Seminoe Lake State Park.

Stretching toward the horizon west of Rawlins is the Great Divide Basin, a gap in the Continental Divide. Part of the basin is covered by the Red Desert, where pronghorn antelopes graze on sage and short grasses. Coyotes, bobcats, and wild horses range in this high desert country, too, as well as prairie dogs, gopher rats, and other rodents.

Rock Springs, on the western edge of the Great Divide Basin, began as an Overland stagecoach stop in 1862. After the Union Pacific arrived and coal was discovered in the area, the town became an important coal-shipping center. Today Rock Springs is still an important center for Wyoming's energy industries.

Just west of Rock Springs is Green River. Loggers used to float logs from the mountains down the river to Green River, where they were shaped into railroad ties for the Union Pacific. Since trona was discovered in the area in 1947, Green River has been known as the Trona Capital of the World. Plants in Green River now process most of the nation's trona into sodium carbonate for baking soda, glass products, and other uses.

From Rock Springs or Green River, vacationers can head south into spectacular Flaming Gorge, given its name by explorer John

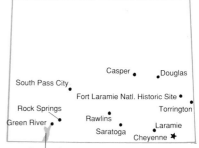

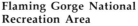

Flaming Gorge Natl. Recreation Area

Flaming Gorge National Recreation Area

Wesley Powell. From the interstate, a loop highway encircles the entire region of sculpted buttes, red-striped canyons, and deep-blue, trout-filled waters. Campgrounds and boat-launching ramps edge Flaming Gorge Reservoir, formed by Flaming Gorge Dam on the Green River in Utah. One of the most awesome sights there is Firehole Canyon, whose chimneylike rock formations tower over the lake.

The Green River area is rendezvous territory, where Rocky Mountain fur trappers had their midsummer meetings. The first was held in July 1825 on Henrys Fork, near the Utah border; a later one, near Granger west of Green River. Mountain man Jim Bridger went on to build Fort Bridger near Blacks Fork. Later rebuilt as a military post, Fort Bridger is now a state historic site. Among its restored buildings are the old guardhouse, the commissary, the commanding officer's Victorian home, and Wyoming's first schoolhouse.

Wyoming's pioneer heritage is preserved at Fort Laramie National Historic Site (left) and at Oregon Trail Ruts National Historic Landmark (right).

ALONG THE OREGON TRAIL

Following the North Platte River, wagons on the Oregon Trail entered Wyoming from Nebraska near Torrington. Today, the town's Homesteaders Museum provides a look into the lives of the pioneers. North of Torrington, near Lusk, are the Spanish Diggings. Early range riders thought these wide pits were Spanish conquistadors' mines. Later research showed they were really quarries where prehistoric Indians mined stone for tools and weapons.

Fort Laramie National Historic Site, northwest of Torrington, is the site of Wyoming's first military post, established to protect the Oregon Trail. Before then, the site was Fort William trading post, Wyoming's first permanent white settlement. Tens of thousands of Oregon Trail emigrants stopped at Fort Laramie for mail, supplies, and repairs.

South of Guernsey is the Oregon Trail Ruts National Historic Landmark. This is a long stretch of the Oregon Trail where thousands of wagon wheels wore deep ruts in the soft sandstone above the North Platte River. Thousands of emigrants carved graffiti and signatures into the walls of nearby Register Cliff. Guernsey State Park's massive museum, perched high on a hill, has stone walls and floors and timber beams. Exhibits there trace residents' interaction with the local environment over the years.

Douglas is the home of the Wyoming State Fair, where Wyomingites exhibit their prize livestock and expert rodeo skills. The Wyoming Pioneers' Memorial Museum is on the state fairgrounds. Northwest of Douglas is Fort Fetterman State Historic Site. Operating from 1867 to 1882, Fort Fetterman was known as a "hardship post." Severe winter weather and the distance from civilization made many of its soldiers desert. The bachelor officers' quarters at Fort Fetterman now house the Fetterman Museum, which traces the fort's history.

Trappers, wagon trains, Indians, and cavalry all left their mark on the Casper area. Mormon Ferry is the spot where Brigham Young established a ferry service in 1847 for his followers along the Mormon Trail. Old Fort Caspar began in 1859 as Platte Bridge Station, a bridge and trading post. After a cavalry company took it over, Lieutenant Caspar Collins was killed there in an Indian attack. The station was renamed Fort Caspar and, through a spelling mistake, the town of Casper got its name. Now the reconstructed fort and its museum offer a glimpse into the area's varied past.

Oil drilling began in the Casper area in 1888, and its first oil refinery was opened in 1895. Casper today is a center for Wyoming's oil and gas industries and its sheep and cattle industries. Hotels, restaurants, convention facilities, and huge recreation and events centers cater to the city's many visitors. Nicolaysen Art Museum is a showplace for many regional western artists. Krampert Theatre, Werner Wildlife Museum, and Tate Mineralogical Museum are on the Casper College campus.

Casper Mountain and Hogadon Basin attract skiers, the North Platte River is filled with trout and pike, and wildlife thrives on the surrounding plains. On the banks of the North Platte east of Casper is Edness Kimball Wilkins State Park, the state's newest park. North of Casper are the Salt Creek oil fields and Teapot Dome, subject of the 1920s political scandal.

On the Sweetwater River southwest of Casper is Independence Rock, which Father De Smet called the "register of the desert." William Sublette gave this giant boulder its name when trappers met there on July 4, 1830. Over five thousand pioneers carved their names in the rock when their wagon trains stopped there to rest.

South Pass City is just a few miles north of South Pass, the wagon trains' gap through the Rocky Mountains. The boomtown sprang up in 1867, when the Carissa Mine struck gold, but folded up again in 1872. Two dozen historic buildings and several living-history demonstrations now attract visitors to South Pass City State Historic Site. Nearby Atlantic City suffered the same boom-and-bust fate. Gold mines—some abandoned and some active—can be seen in the area.

CENTRAL WYOMING

Most of the Wind River mountains and basin are within the Wind River Indian Reservation, home of the Eastern Shoshone and Northern Arapahoe Indians. Shoshone chief Washakie used to call the mountains' east slope the "Valley of the Warm Winds."

Upper Green River Lake in the Wind River Mountains

Chief Washakie is buried in Fort Washakie's military cemetery. Sacajawea, the Shoshone guide for the Lewis and Clark Expedition, is buried west of there.

Lander and Riverton are the largest towns in the Wind River region. Captain Bonneville discovered oil near Lander in the 1830s, and Wyoming's first oil well was drilled there in 1883, in what is called the Dallas Field. In Sinks Canyon State Park, southwest of Lander, the Popo Agie River disappears into a cave and shows up half a mile (0.8 kilometer) away.

Riverton is surrounded by rich agricultural land that the federal government took back from the reservation for homesteading. North of Riverton, Boysen Reservoir in Boysen State Park is a popular swimming, boating, and camping spot.

As the Wind River flows between the Owl Creek and Bridger

Devils Tower, the nation's first national monument, is the core of an extinct volcano.

mountains, it courses through beautiful Wind River Canyon, a scenic gorge over 2,000 feet (610 meters) deep. Signs along the highway tell the type and geological period of each rock formation. Once the river leaves the canyon to the north, its name changes to the Bighorn.

At the north end of the canyon is Thermopolis, whose name combines the Latin word *thermae* ("heat") and the Greek word *polis* ("city"). Hot Springs State Park, on the edge of town, surrounds the largest mineral hot springs in the world. The steaming mineral waters gush from the earth in a constant flood. As the water streams over rock terraces, its minerals color them yellow, red, and orange. The waters are channeled into both public and private swimming pools and bathhouses.

THE POWDER RIVER AND BIGHORN BASINS

The Sioux Indians gazed with reverence and awe upon the Black Hills east of the Powder River Basin. The hills, spilling over from western South Dakota, are not really black. They appear dark because they are covered so densely with ponderosa pines. Wyoming's largest concentration of white-tailed deer live in the Black Hills, as well as wild turkeys, elk, and mule deer. Looming over the Belle Fourche River at the hills' western edge is Devils Tower, the nation's first national monument. This stump-shaped rock formation, rising 1,280 feet (390 meters), is the core of an extinct volcano. Keyhole State Park, west of the Black Hills near Interstate 90, is a recreation area where visitors enjoy boating, fishing, and wildlife watching.

Soldiers at Fort Phil Kearny, on the east slope of the Bighorn Mountains, fought dozens of battles with thousands of Indians to protect the Bozeman Trail. Today the fort, along with the Fetterman and Wagon Box battle sites, is a state historic site. Farther up the trail, on the Tongue River, is the Connor Battlefield, site of the 1865 Battle of Tongue River.

The Bighorn Basin is like a great bowl-shaped fortress surrounded by mountains. Free from the Indian battles that ravaged the other side of the Bighorns, this basin was ranching territory. To the north, Montana's Yellowtail Dam has formed Bighorn Lake within Bighorn Canyon; both are partly in Montana and partly in Wyoming. As the Bighorn River slices through the mountains, it passes spectacular, layered cliffs rich with fossils.

More than two hundred wild horses roam through the Pryor Mountain Wild Horse Range north and east of Lovell. In the mountains west of Burgess Junction is a mysterious "medicine wheel." Prehistoric Indians built this circle of white stones, 245 feet (75 meters) in circumference, with twenty-eight spokes radiating from the center. Though there are many theories, including one that it is a prehistoric calendar, no one knows just why it was built.

The Scout, **a statue
of Buffalo Bill in Cody**

Dinosaur fossils, Indian remains, and semiprecious stones are hidden in the rock and clay of the badlands around Greybull. Many of the findings are displayed in the Greybull Museum.

Bradford Brinton Memorial Ranch, south of Sheridan, is a twenty-room ranch house that houses an art museum. Besides an extensive western art collection, the memorial holds many rare books and documents. The Trail End Historic Center in Sheridan is housed in a beautifully crafted Flemish-style mansion that was the home of Wyoming governor and senator John B. Kendrick. In 1913, after driving many cattle herds into Wyoming, Kendrick made this the end of his trail and settled down. He brought in many species of trees from all over the state to shade his grounds.

On the west slope of the Bighorn Mountains near Hyattville is Medicine Lodge State Archaeological Site. While many of the site's prehistoric treasures lie underground, Indian petroglyphs and pictographs are visible on the red-sandstone cliff walls.

Cody, on the Shoshone River, was founded by the legendary Buffalo Bill. The Buffalo Bill Historical Center is four museums in one: the Plains Indian Museum, the Whitney Gallery of Western Art, the Winchester Museum, and the Buffalo Bill Museum. In 1902, Cody spent $80,000 building the beautifully preserved Irma Hotel, named for his second daughter.

The historic mural in Cody's Church of Jesus Christ of Latter-day Saints covers the entire domed ceiling of the 36-foot (11-meter) chapel foyer. Artifacts and historic photographs there tell the story of Mormon settlers in the Bighorn Basin. Old Trail Town, on the western edge of town, is a reconstruction of Old Cody City.

YELLOWSTONE, GRAND TETON, AND JACKSON HOLE

The highway west of Cody through Shoshone National Forest follows the Shoshone River, once named Stinkingwater for its sulphurous odor. This road is the east entrance to Yellowstone National Park, the world's oldest national park. Yellowstone's ten thousand thermal (heat-related) features include hot, bubbling mineral pools, mudpots and mud volcanoes, steaming holes, and geysers—streams of hot water shooting into the sky. Molten rock not far below the earth's surface is the source of all the heat and steam.

There are more geysers in Yellowstone than anywhere else in the world. Old Faithful is the most famous of the geysers. For over a century, it has erupted twenty-one to twenty-three times a day, blasting water more than 100 feet (30 meters) into the air. At the park's Mammoth Hot Springs are tier upon tier of mineral-hued stone terraces. Norris Geyser Basin and the Firehole River Geyser Basin contain the park's largest collection of geysers. Steamboat, the world's tallest geyser, erupts as high as 400 feet (122 meters) in Norris basin.

Among Yellowstone's ten thousand thermal features are hot springs (above) and the geyser known as Old Faithful (right).

Yellowstone's wildlife is spectacular, too. Moose, black bears, grizzly bears, bison, elk, coyotes, pronghorn antelope, and bighorn sheep wander freely through the rugged park. Bald eagles, gulls, ospreys, pelicans, and rare trumpeter swans nest around Yellowstone Lake and other watery areas. In the underbrush are chipmunks, pocket gophers, porcupines, muskrats, and mice.

The Yellowstone River's Upper and Lower falls cascade through the Grand Canyon of the Yellowstone, sending foam and mist high into the air. At its lowest point, the canyon is 1,540 feet (469 meters) deep. Artist Point and Inspiration Point offer scenic

Above: Jackson Lake and Mount Moran in Grand Teton National Park

views of the falls and the grey, pink, and purple canyon walls.

The John D. Rockefeller, Jr. Memorial Parkway leads south from Yellowstone into Grand Teton National Park, whose scenery is nothing less than breathtaking. Within the park, Jackson Lake and Jenny Lake lie in the shadow of the spectacular, snowcapped Grand Teton range. Elk and moose abound in the park, often meeting up with humans along hiking trails, horse paths, or trout-fishing banks.

South of Grand Teton park is Jackson Hole, a high basin surrounded on all sides by mountain ranges. Indians hunted, trappers trapped, surveyors mapped, and homesteaders settled in this long, narrow valley rich with wild game. Today, the community of Jackson bustles with tourist-industry trades. From Jackson, it's a short jaunt to the Snow King Mountain and Teton Village ski resorts, the National Elk Refuge, and the area's many dude ranches. Jackson is also the headquarters for Bridger-Teton National Forest, a vast wilderness covering nearly 3.5 million acres (1.4 million hectares).

Besides serving tourists, Jackson has an identity of its own. The sidewalks are boardwalks with rough-hewn wooden rails. People enter the city square through arches made of elk antlers. In the square are memorials to local veterans of several wars. Here, too, Boy Scouts sell antlers they have collected from the elk refuge every year. Jackson's Wildlife of the American West Art Museum has the country's finest collection of wildlife art.

WESTERN WYOMING

From Hoback Junction, south of Jackson, highways branch southwest and southeast. The eastern branch winds along the Hoback River through scenic Hoback Canyon, eventually crossing the Green River. Between Daniel and Pinedale are two momentous sites. One is the Father De Smet Monument, where the missionary held the first Catholic Mass in Wyoming. The other is Trapper's Point National Historic Site, the rendezvous area where trappers met for many of their summertime gatherings. From Daniel, the highway parallels the Green River. From Pinedale, another road heads to Big Sandy Recreation Area and into the Great Divide Basin.

The west fork from Hoback Junction follows the Grand Canyon of the Snake River into the Star Valley. This lush dairy country, often called Little Switzerland, produces more cheese than

An old barn in Grand Teton National Park

anywhere else in Wyoming. Farther south is Fossil Butte National Monument. Embedded in this 1,000-foot (305-meter) geological formation are the world's largest deposits of fossilized fish, some as old as fifty million years. In nearby Kemmerer is the Fossil Country Frontier Museum. In 1902, J. C. Penney opened his first variety store in Kemmerer, and the J. C. Penney Historical Foundation maintains his old homestead there.

Penney's store took in $29,000 in its first year—an amazing sum for the times. In his own way, Penney joined the ranks of Wyoming's many visionary pioneering spirits—people such as Jim Bridger, Esther Morris, Nellie Ross, and Buffalo Bill Cody—whose creative ventures helped shape the nation and make Wyoming the proud land it is today.

FACTS AT A GLANCE

GENERAL INFORMATION

Statehood: July 10, 1890, forty-fourth state

Origin of Name: The name Wyoming is derived from the Delaware Indian phrase *meche-weami-ing*, meaning "land of mountains and valleys alternating."

State Capital: Cheyenne

State Nickname: Equality State is Wyoming's official nickname. Unofficially, Wyoming is also known as the Cowboy State.

State Flag: Wyoming's state flag features the white silhouette of a bison on a field of blue. Within the bison emblem is the state seal, rendered in blue and white. A border of white inside a border of red surrounds the field of blue. Verna Keays (later to become Mrs. A. C. Keyes) of Buffalo designed the flag, and the state legislature officially adopted it on January 31, 1917. According to Mrs. Keyes's description, the red border represents Wyoming's Indians and the blood of toiling pioneers, the white band signifies purity and uprightness, and the blue field represents Wyoming's blue skies and distant mountains.

State Motto: "Equal Rights"

State Bird: Meadowlark

State Flower: Indian paintbrush

State Tree: Plains cottonwood

State Gemstone: Jade

State Mammal: Bison

State Song: "Wyoming," words by Charles E. Winter and music by G. E. Knapp, adopted as the official state song in 1955:

> In the far and mighty West,
> Where the crimson sun seeks rest,
> There's a growing splendid State that lies above
> On the breast of this great land;
> Where the massive Rockies stand,
> There's Wyoming young and strong, the State I love!

Chorus:

Wyoming, Wyoming! Land of the sunlight clear!
Wyoming, Wyoming! Land that we hold so dear!
Wyoming, Wyoming! Precious art thou and thine;
Wyoming, Wyoming! Beloved State of mine!

In thy flowers wild and sweet,
Colors rare and perfumes meet;
There's the columbine so pure, the daisy too,
Wild the rose and red it springs,
White the button and its rings,
Thou art loyal for they're red and white and blue.

(Chorus)

Where thy peaks with crowned head,
Rising till the sky they wed,
Sit like snow queens ruling wood and stream and plain;
'Neath thy granite bases deep,
'Neath thy bosom's broadened sweep,
Lie the riches that have gained and brought thee fame.

(Chorus)

Other treasures thou dost hold,
Men and women thou dost mould;
True and earnest are the lives that thou dost raise;
Strength thy children thou dost teach,
Nature's truth thou givst to each,
Free and noble are thy workings and thy ways.

(Chorus)

In the nation's banner free
There's one star that has for me
A radiance pure and a splendor like the sun;
Mine it is, Wyoming's star,
Home it leads me, near or far;
O Wyoming! all my heart and love you've won!

(Chorus)

POPULATION

Population: 453,588, fiftieth among the states (1990 census)

Population Density: 5 people per sq. mi. (2 people per km²)

Population Distribution: 63 percent of the people live in cities or towns.

```
Cheyenne . . . . . . . . . . . . . . . . . . . . . . . . . . . . . . . . . . . . . . . . . . . . . 50,008
Casper . . . . . . . . . . . . . . . . . . . . . . . . . . . . . . . . . . . . . . . . . . . . . . . 46,742
Laramie . . . . . . . . . . . . . . . . . . . . . . . . . . . . . . . . . . . . . . . . . . . . . . 26,687
Rock Springs. . . . . . . . . . . . . . . . . . . . . . . . . . . . . . . . . . . . . . . . . . 19,050
Gillette. . . . . . . . . . . . . . . . . . . . . . . . . . . . . . . . . . . . . . . . . . . . . . . 17,635
Sheridan . . . . . . . . . . . . . . . . . . . . . . . . . . . . . . . . . . . . . . . . . . . . . 13,900
Green River. . . . . . . . . . . . . . . . . . . . . . . . . . . . . . . . . . . . . . . . . . . . 12,711
```
(Population figures according to 1990 census)

Population Growth: Wyoming's population has undergone several spurts of growth since territorial days. Because of ranching and homesteading opportunities, population more than doubled in the 1870s and then tripled in the 1880s. Higher-than-average growth continued into the first decade of the twentieth century. After that, the state's population growth leveled off to a steady, more gradual rise. Between 1970 and 1980, new energy-industry jobs caused Wyoming's population to grow more than 41 percent, making it the third-fastest-growing state in the nation. In 1980, Wyoming ranked forty-ninth among the states in population, while Alaska ranked fiftieth. A decline in the state's petroleum industry in the early 1980s slowed population growth, however, and Wyoming had dropped to fiftieth place in number of residents by 1990. The list below shows population growth in Wyoming since 1870:

Year	Population
1870	9,118
1880	20,789
1890	62,555
1900	92,531
1910	145,965
1920	194,402
1930	225,565
1940	250,742
1950	290,529
1960	330,066
1970	332,416
1980	469,557
1990	453,588

GEOGRAPHY

Borders: Wyoming is bordered on the north by Montana and on the west by Idaho, Utah, and a small section of Montana. Utah and Colorado border Wyoming on the south. On the east, Wyoming is bordered by South Dakota and Nebraska.

Highest Point: Gannett Peak, 13,804 ft. (4,207 m)

Lowest Point: Belle Fourche River in Crook County, 3,100 ft. (945 m) above sea level

Yellowstone Lower Falls in the Grand Canyon of the Yellowstone River

Greatest Distances: North to south—275 mi. (443 km)
East to west—362 mi. (583 km)

Area: 97,809 sq. mi. (253,325 km²)

Rank in Area Among the States: Ninth

Rivers: In Wyoming are the headwaters of three of the nation's major river systems: the Missouri, the Colorado, and the Columbia. The Missouri River and its tributaries drain 72 percent of Wyoming's land area, the Colorado River system drains over 21 percent of the state, and the Columbia system drains over 5 percent. Northwest Wyoming's Yellowstone River is a major tributary of the Missouri River, whose waters, in turn, pour into the great Mississippi River. The Yellowstone's Grand Canyon and falls are among the most spectacular sights in Yellowstone National Park. Tributaries of the Yellowstone, flowing north to join the Yellowstone in Montana, include the Clarks Fork, Bighorn, Tongue, and Powder rivers. South of Thermopolis, the Bighorn's name changes to the Wind River, whose waters have formed Wind River Canyon.

The Shoshone River, a branch of the Bighorn, has cut a deep canyon through Shoshone National Forest east of Yellowstone park. The Belle Fourche and Little Missouri rivers, in northeast Wyoming, are direct tributaries of the Missouri River. Fed by many tributary creeks, the Cheyenne River and its South Fork drain east-central Wyoming on their eastward course to the Missouri.

The North Platte River drains the southeastern quarter of the state as it, too, flows eastward to join the Missouri. Major tributaries of the North Platte are the Laramie and Medicine Bow rivers in the southeast and the Sweetwater River, which flows through the hills of south-central Wyoming.

The major waterway in the southwestern part of the state is the Green River. It flows southward into Utah, widening into Flaming Gorge Reservoir near the border and eventually emptying into the Colorado River. The Snake River rises in the Absaroka Mountains and crosses Yellowstone National Park, cutting a scenic canyon as it flows south through Grand Teton National Park. It then flows westward into Idaho, finally pouring into the Columbia River.

Lakes: The largest of Wyoming's natural lakes are Yellowstone and Shoshone lakes in Yellowstone National Park and Jackson Lake in Grand Teton National Park. Other natural lakes include Lewis, Heart, and Fremont lakes. Artificial lakes, created by damming rivers, include Pathfinder, Alcova, Seminoe, Glendo, and Guernsey reservoirs on the North Platte River; Keyhole Reservoir on the Belle Fourche River; Buffalo Bill Reservoir on the Shoshone River; Grayrocks on the Laramie River; and Boysen Reservoir on the Wind River. Bighorn Lake, which extends northward over the Montana border, is formed by Montana's Yellowtail Dam. Flaming Gorge Reservoir, which continues into Utah on the Green River, is created by Utah's Flaming Gorge Dam.

Topography: Wyoming straddles both the Rocky Mountain and the Great Plains regions of the United States. In addition, a small portion of its southwest corner is part of the Great Basin region.

With its many mountain ranges, Wyoming's average elevation is 6,700 ft. (2,042 m), the second-highest elevation among the fifty states, after Colorado's. Meandering from northwest to south-central Wyoming is the Continental Divide. This string of peaks marks the dividing line between the country's westward-flowing and eastward-flowing rivers.

Mountain ranges along Wyoming's western border include the Teton, Gros Ventre, Snake River, Salt River, and Wyoming ranges. Grand Teton, the state's second-highest peak, is in the Teton Range. The Absaroka Range sweeps down from Montana into northwestern Wyoming. As the Absarokas extend southward, they are joined by the Owl Creek and Bridger mountains, which form the bottom of a great loop. The Bighorn Mountains form the eastern arm of that loop, extending northward to the Montana border. The lowlands within the loop are called the Bighorn Basin.

Continuing south and east from the Absarokas is the Wind River Range, whose lofty peaks include Gannett Peak, the state's highest point. The Rattlesnake Hills,

Green Mountains, and Ferris Mountains rise farther east. North of these ranges lie the Wind River Basin and the Shoshone Basin, and to the south is the Great Divide Basin. This area marks a break in the Continental Divide. Waters in this dusty, treeless region flow neither west nor east; they remain within the basin and quickly evaporate. The Laramie, Medicine Bow, and Sierra Madre mountains extend into southeastern Wyoming from Colorado.

East of the Bighorn and Laramie mountains are Wyoming's Great Plains. The plains in the northern part of the state are also called Thunder Basin. Cattle and sheep graze on the grasses and other small plants that grow on the state's high, rolling plains. Irrigation has allowed the plains to produce corn, beans, sugar beets, hay, barley, and other crops. Spilling over the northeastern border from South Dakota are the buttes and strange rock formations of the Black Hills. Here rises Devils Tower, the core of an ancient, extinct volcano.

Climate: In general, Wyoming has a cool, dry climate. The dry air makes the winters' cold temperatures feel less severe. Wyoming's diverse terrain and varying elevations make for regional variations in temperature and precipitation (rain, melted snow, and other moisture). The state's average temperature in January is 19° F. (-7° C), while January temperatures in the mountainous Yellowstone Park region average 12° F. (-11° C). Lower-lying Casper averages 22° F. (-6° C) in January. High in Wyoming's mountains, temperatures may drop below freezing any time of the year. In July, the average temperature statewide is 67° F. (19° C). The Yellowstone region's average July temperature, however, is a cool 59° F. (15° C), while Casper's July average is 71° F. (22° C). The highest temperature ever recorded in Wyoming was 115° F. (46° C), measured in Basin on August 8, 1983, and at Diversion Dam on July 15, 1988. Moran registered the state's lowest temperature, -63° F. (-53° C), on February 9, 1933.

Overall, the state's average rainfall is 14.5 in. (37 cm) per year. The average rainfall in different regions of the state, however, ranges from 5 to 50 in. (13 to 127 cm) a year. Snow caps the tops of some of Wyoming's highest peaks all year round. The heaviest snowfall occurs in the mountainous northwest, which averages about 260 in. (660 cm) of snow a year. The Bighorn Basin, in contrast, receives only about 15 to 20 in. (38 to 51 cm) of snowfall a year.

NATURE

Trees: Alders, ashes, limber pines, lodgepole pines, ponderosa pines, white pines, yellow pines, alpine firs, Douglas firs, Engelmann spruces, aspens, mountain mahoganies, birches, cottonwoods, hawthorns, poplars, whitebarks, willows

Wild Plants: Arnicas, Indian paintbrush, bluegrass, sagebrush, buffalo grass, buttercups, cacti, cowslips, currants, evening stars, tufted fescue, five-fingers, shooting stars, flax, forget-me-nots, globeflowers, serviceberries, goldenrod, columbines, gooseberries, greasewood, Jacob's ladders, junipers, kinnikinnick, lichens, mosses, raspberries, fireweed, redtops, saltbush, wheatgrass, saxifrage, sour dock, violets, windflowers, yucca, larkspurs

Animals: Pronghorn antelopes, white-tailed deer, mule deer, badgers, moose, lynxes, black bears, grizzly bears, beavers, cottontail rabbits, bison, coyotes, garter snakes, elk, ferrets, foxes, Rocky Mountain goats, pocket gophers, snowshoe hares, jackrabbits, porcupines, lizards, marmots, martens, field mice, Rocky Mountain jumping mice, moles, bullsnakes, muskrats, bobcats, otters, pikas, snowshoe rabbits, raccoons, kangaroo rats, wood rats, chipmunks, prairie rattlesnakes, bighorn sheep, skunks, red squirrels, northern flying squirrels, ground squirrels, voles, wildcats, wolverines, mountain lions, prairie dogs

Birds: Chickadees, grouse, coots, cranes, partridges, doves, ducks, bald and golden eagles, prairie falcons, Canada and other geese, snipes, grackles, gulls, gyrfalcons, hawks, jays, ospreys, juncoes, magpies, warblers, mockingbirds, nuthatches, orioles, owls, white pelicans, pheasants, rails, sparrows, brown thrashers, thrushes, trumpeter swans, wild turkeys, woodpeckers, wrens

Fish: Bass, trout (rainbow, brook, cutthroat, brown, golden, and lake), crappie, bluegill, ling, perch, sauger (sand pike), northern pike, sunfish, walleye, catfish, mountain whitefish (grayling)

GOVERNMENT

The government of Wyoming, like the federal government, is divided into three branches: legislative, executive, and judicial. The state legislature makes the state laws. Like the U.S. Congress, Wyoming's legislature consists of two houses: a senate and a house of representatives. State legislators are elected by voters in Wyoming's senatorial and representative districts. The thirty state senators are elected to four-year terms, and the sixty-four state representatives serve two-year terms. Wyoming's legislature meets every year. After the legislature passes a bill into law, the governor either approves or vetoes it. By a two-thirds vote in both houses, the legislature can override the governor's veto.

The governor is the head of the executive branch, which enforces state laws. Voters elect the governor to a four-year term, and the governor may be re-elected an unlimited number of times. Other executive officers, all elected to four-year terms, are the secretary of state, state auditor, state superintendent of public instruction, and state treasurer. Except for the treasurer, these officers may serve an unlimited number of terms. Wyoming has no office of lieutenant governor, as do many other states. A vacancy in the governorship is filled by the secretary of state until the next election. The governor appoints the attorney general and the heads of the budget and personnel departments.

The judicial branch interprets the law and tries cases. The state's highest court is the supreme court. Its primary function is to hear appeals from lower courts in the state. The five supreme court justices preside for eight-year terms and choose one of their members to serve as chief justice. They are appointed by the governor from among nominees submitted by the Wyoming Judicial Nominating Commission.

One or two judges, serving six-year terms, preside in each of Wyoming's nine district courts. They, too, are nominated for their positions and appointed by the governor. District judges try major civil and criminal cases and also hear appeals from some lower courts. At the local level, there are county courts, police courts, municipal courts, and justice-of-the-peace courts.

Wyoming's state constitution has been in effect since 1890. It has been amended, or changed, fifty-one times. To amend the constitution or to call a constitutional convention requires a two-thirds vote in both houses of the legislature and a majority of the popular vote.

A three- to five-member board of commissioners governs each of Wyoming's twenty-three counties. Commissioners are elected to four-year terms. Communities with populations of 4,000 or more are called cities, and those with 150 to 4,000 residents are classified as towns. The mayor-council form of city government is the most common in Wyoming.

Number of Counties: 23

U.S. Representatives: 1

Electoral Votes: 3

Voting Qualifications: Eighteen years of age, state resident for one year, county resident for sixty days, and district resident for ten days

EDUCATION

William Vaux, the chaplain at Fort Laramie, opened Wyoming's first school in 1852. Other schools were opened at Fort Bridger in 1860 and Cheyenne in 1868. In 1869, the territorial legislature instituted taxes to support public schools. Wyoming Territory's first high school opened in 1875. A state board of education was established in 1919.

Wyoming state law requires children to attend school from age seven until age sixteen or until one completes eighth grade. In the late 1980s, about 99,000 students were enrolled in Wyoming's public elementary and secondary schools. There are also a number of parochial elementary and secondary schools in the state, most of them in Cheyenne or on the Wind River Indian Reservation.

The average educational level statewide is 12.6 years of schooling. About 78 percent of the adults in Wyoming are high-school graduates, and 17 percent are college graduates. The state's literacy rate is high, ranking fourth in the nation. Wyoming's state expenditure for education per student is among the highest in the United States. Both property taxes and proceeds from activities on state-owned lands go toward education.

Founded in 1886 and opened the following year, the University of Wyoming in Laramie is the state's only public university. Wyoming also supports seven public community colleges. They are located in Casper, Riverton, Torrington, Powell, Sheridan, Rock Springs, and Cheyenne.

ECONOMY AND INDUSTRY

Principal Products:

Agriculture: Beef cattle, sheep, lambs, dairy products, sugar beets, dry beans, barley, potatoes, alfalfa, hay, oats, winter wheat, chickens, hogs, corn, honey

Manufacturing: Aeronautics equipment, beet sugar, meat products, flour, petroleum and coal products, copper products, aluminum products, chemicals, farm machinery, fabricated metal products, fertilizers, food products, clothing, printed materials, cement, stone and clay products, glass products

Natural Resources: Bentonite, soda ash (trona), uranium, coal, petroleum, natural gas, iron ore, gypsum, feldspar, agate, jade, limestone, crushed stone, sand, gravel, grasslands

Business and Trade: Mining is Wyoming's principal industry, accounting for about 26 percent of the gross state product, or GSP (the annual value of all goods and services produced in the state), and employing 10 percent of Wyoming's workers. About half the state's labor force works in service industries. Government is the largest service-industry employer, accounting for about 18 percent of the gross state product and employing almost one-fourth of the state's workers. Transportation, communication, and public utilities account for about 12 percent of the GSP; wholesale and retail trade produce another 12 percent; and finance, insurance, and real estate generate about 8 percent. Other important service industries in Wyoming include community, social, and personal services such as private schools and hospitals, hotels, advertising, and data-processing services. Manufacturing, construction, and agriculture together add another 12 percent to Wyoming's GSP.

Communication: Wyoming's first newspaper was the *Daily Telegraph*, which began publication at Fort Bridger in 1863. Today, about forty-five newspapers are published in Wyoming, ten of them daily papers. Those with the largest circulations are Casper's *Star Tribune* and Cheyenne's *Wyoming State Tribune* and *Wyoming Eagle*. Wyoming's first radio station was KDFN (now KTWO), which began broadcasting from Casper in 1930. The state's first television station was Cheyenne's KFBC, which began operation in 1954. Today, eight television stations and about sixty radio stations are broadcast in Wyoming.

Transportation: About 39,500 mi. (63,567 km) of roadways pass through Wyoming, and about three-fifths of that mileage is paved. Interstate 80, in southern Wyoming, spans the entire width of the state, roughly paralleling the route of the Union Pacific Railroad. Interstate 25 is the major north-south route, entering southeastern Wyoming from Colorado and passing through Cheyenne and Casper to Buffalo, where it joins Interstate 90. Interstate 90 follows an east-west route from northeastern Wyoming and, from Buffalo, continues north through Sheridan into Montana. The state highway system maintains excellent roads throughout the state. Several state and U.S. highways facilitate travel through the mountainous central, northern, and western parts of Wyoming. A number of scenic roads pass through Wyoming's mountains and forests. The Happy Jack Road, or State Highway 210, is a 38-mi. (61-km) route between Cheyenne and Laramie. It passes pine forests and towering rock formations in the Pole Mountain area of Medicine Bow National

Forest. State Highway 130 is a scenic highway west of Laramie through the Medicine Bow Mountains. Like many of Wyoming's mountain roads and passes, it is closed in the winter.

Wyoming's first railroad was the Union Pacific Railroad, which entered southeastern Wyoming in 1867. As the tracks moved west, each new "farthest-west" point gave rise to a booming railroad town. Cheyenne, Laramie, Rawlins, and Evanston all began as railroad towns along the Union Pacific line. Chicago & North Western railroad service reached Casper in 1888, and the Chicago, Burlington & Quincy Railroad began runs to Casper in 1913. Today, about 2,400 mi. (3,862 km) of railroad track cross the state. About ninety airports serve Wyoming's cities and towns. The airports at Casper and Cheyenne, served by three major airlines, are the state's busiest commercial air facilities.

SOCIAL AND CULTURAL LIFE

Museums: Most of Wyoming's museums highlight Indian and pioneer history and culture. The Wyoming State Museum in Cheyenne displays artifacts, rafts, household items, and cultural exhibits relating to Plains Indians, mountain men, and pioneers. It also houses an art gallery. The Cheyenne Frontier Days Old West Museum in Cheyenne is one of the finest museums in the Rocky Mountain region. Its several sections include the Carriage Room, displaying over thirty of the museum's 126 coaches and carriages; the Frontier Days Hall of Fame Room, displaying rodeo memorabilia; the Old West Room, with replicas of historic building interiors; the Union Pacific Room, highlighting Wyoming's railroad history; and the Indian Room, honoring legendary Indians and their deeds.

The military museum at Cheyenne's F. E. Warren Air Force Base traces the history of the old fort and the modern base from 1876 to the present. In Pine Bluffs, the Texas Trail Museum and park memorialize the various waves of people that have migrated through and developed this area throughout its history. In Laramie, the University of Wyoming's geological museum displays fossils, rocks, and minerals. Housed in the Coe Library is the American Heritage Center, one of the best research institutions in the western United States. The Laramie Plains Museum, in the Ivinson Mansion, houses pioneer families' artifacts. In Rawlins is the Wyoming Frontier Prison Museum. Fossils of southwestern Wyoming are on display at Western Wyoming College Natural History Museum in Rock Springs. Fort Bridger State Museum in Fort Bridger displays artifacts from Fort Bridger's varied past.

In Casper, the Nicolaysen Art Museum highlights both regional and national contemporary artists. Casper College's Tate Mineralogical Museum displays rocks, minerals, fossils, and Wyoming jade. Casper's Werner Wildlife Museum features African and Wyoming mammals. Exhibits at the Fort Caspar Museum trace the social and natural history of central Wyoming.

The Indian Heritage Center on the Wind River Indian Reservation displays Arapahoe beadwork and other artifacts. The Riverton Museum exhibits Shoshone and Arapahoe folk arts and outlines the history of the reservation. The Johnson County/Jim Gatchell Museum in Buffalo specializes in Bozeman Trail history. The Bradford Brinton Memorial Museum in Big Horn features western art and history

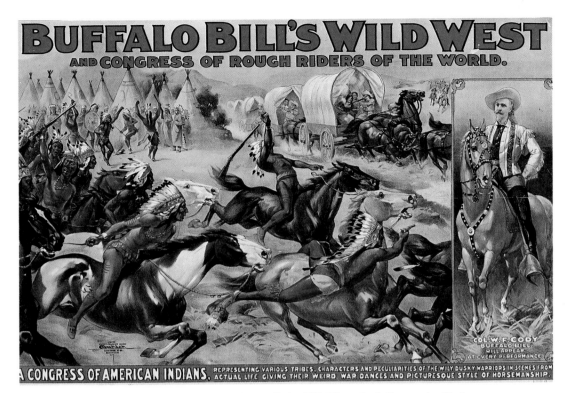

Posters such as this are on display at the Buffalo Bill Historical Center in Cody.

collections within the setting of an authentic ranch. In Douglas are the Wyoming Pioneers' Memorial Museum and Fort Fetterman State Historic Site's museum.

The Buffalo Bill Historical Center in Cody houses four museums: the Buffalo Bill Museum, a collection of thousands of items of Cody memorabilia; the Whitney Gallery of Western Art, with original works by Charles M. Russell, Albert Bierstadt, Frederic Remington, Karl Bodmer, and many others; the Plains Indian Museum, displaying Sioux, Cheyenne, Shoshone, Crow, Arapahoe, and Blackfeet artifacts; and the Winchester Museum, containing over five thousand firearms. The Wildlife of the American West Art Gallery in Jackson is the world's finest collection of wildlife art. Among Jackson's many other museums and galleries are the Jackson Hole Museum, the Wax Museum of Old Wyoming, and Teton County Historical Center. The National Park Service operates the Fur Trade Museum and the Colter Bay Indian Arts Museum in Grand Teton National Park. It also has natural history museums at Devils Tower National Monument and Yellowstone National Park. The Museum of the Mountain Men in Pinedale offers memorabilia from the days of western Wyoming's mountain men.

Libraries: The University of Wyoming's William Robertson Coe Library, with 1 million volumes, is the largest library in the state. The American Heritage Center, a separate administrative unit housed at the Coe Library, has an extensive western history collection. The campus also has a geology library. Wyoming's second-largest library is the State Library in Cheyenne, which began as the Wyoming Territorial Library in 1871. The State Library contains a sizable law-book collection. Each of Wyoming's twenty-three counties maintains a public library.

Performing Arts: Classical music is presented by the Cheyenne Symphony Orchestra, the Casper Civic Symphony Orchestra, and the University of Wyoming music department. In addition, nationally famous ensembles and soloists appear regularly in Wyoming concert halls. Every summer, Wyoming's Western Arts Trio performs in Laramie, Cheyenne, and Saratoga. The Grand Teton Music Festival in Jackson Hole is perhaps Wyoming's most extravagant musical event. Through July and August, renowned composers, conductors, and instrumentalists converge at the base of the Tetons to present concerts, lectures, workshops, and master classes. Jazz, folk, and ethnic music can be heard throughout the state. There are polka festivals in Rock Springs and Sheridan; bluegrass festivals in Curt Gowdy State Park, Fort Bridger, Gillette, and Sheridan; a Basque festival near Buffalo; and the Yellowstone Jazz Festival in Cody. Community theater groups perform in Casper, Cody, Sheridan, Lander, and Cheyenne. Melodramas are presented in Cheyenne, Cody, and Jackson. In Cheyenne, Riverton, and Evanston, drama is brought to young people through community children's theaters.

Sports and Recreation: Wyoming's national and state parklands and recreation areas attract campers, fishermen, hunters, boaters, mountain climbers, rock hunters, hikers, bicycle riders, horseback riders, and wildlife watchers. Yellowstone and Grand Teton national parks are Wyoming's most famous, and most visited, scenic attractions. Yellowstone, the nation's oldest and world's largest national park, encompasses such thermal phenomena as geysers and bubbling mineral springs. The spectacular canyon and falls of the Yellowstone River are also within the park. Adjoining Yellowstone to the south is Grand Teton National Park, with its majestic, snow-covered peaks, abundant wildlife, and sparkling lakes. Other national areas in Wyoming are Bighorn Canyon National Recreation Area (which extends into Montana), Flaming Gorge National Recreation Area (which extends into Utah), Devils Tower and Fossil Butte national monuments, and Fort Laramie National Historic Site.

Wyoming has nine national forests. Four of them lie wholly within Wyoming: Bridger-Teton, Shoshone, Medicine Bow, and Bighorn. Five others lie partly in other states. Black Hills National Forest extends into South Dakota; Caribou, into Utah and Idaho; Targhee, into Idaho; and Ashley and Wasatch, into Utah. Thunder Basin National Grassland is administered under Medicine Bow National Forest.

The state of Wyoming operates Big Sandy State Recreation Area and twelve state parks. Boysen State Park is the state's largest, and Hot Springs State Park, with the world's largest hot springs, is the most visited. The other state parks are Bear River, Buffalo Bill, Curt Gowdy, Edness Kimball Wilkins, Glendo, Guernsey, Keyhole, Medicine Lodge, Seminoe, and Sinks Canyon.

Hikers may take a number of designated trails in Wyoming's wilderness areas, and float trippers take advantage of the Shoshone, Snake, and Salt rivers. Horseback-riding trails wind through Grand Teton National Park. Wyoming's wildlife refuges include the National Elk Refuge near Jackson and Jackson Hole Wildlife Park near Moran Junction.

Wyoming's most popular ski slopes are in the Jackson area and include the Grand Targhee and Snow King ski areas. Skiers also enjoy Sleeping Giant, west of Cody; Eagle Rock, east of Evanston; High Park, in Bighorn National Forest; Hogadon, on Casper Mountain; Snowy Range, in Medicine Bow National Forest;

Pine Creek, east of Cokeville; Bighorn/Greybull, east of Greybull; Sundance Mountains near Newcastle; and Snowshoe Hollow, east of Afton. Snowmobiling, sleigh riding, and cutter racing are some other popular wintertime sports.

Dude ranches all over the state provide a taste of Western living. Some furnish their visitors with luxurious resort lodges, while others put their guests to work. Wyoming's *volksmarches* are 10-km (6.2-mi.) walks along state park trails. Volksmarchers in the state are affiliated with other brisk walkers through national and international volksmarchers' associations.

Historic Sites and Landmarks:

Fort Bridger State Historic Site, near Fort Bridger, preserves the trading post that was built in 1842 by Jim Bridger and served as an important stopover for westward-bound emigrants. Several buildings from the fort's military-post era (1858-90) have been restored.

Fort Fetterman State Historic Site, near Douglas, recalls the history of this "hardship post" through a museum in the old officers' quarters.

Fort Fred Steele State Historic Site, east of Rawlins, preserves some of the structures of a fort built to protect railroad workers from Indians.

Fort Laramie National Historic Site, northwest of Torrington, is the site of Wyoming's first military post, established to protect travelers along Oregon Trail; and the site of the earlier Fort William, the trading post that was Wyoming's first permanent white settlement.

Fort Phil Kearny State Historic Site, north of Buffalo, encompasses the sites of the Fetterman Fight, the Wagon Box Fight, and the 1866 fort that protected the Bozeman Trail.

Independence Rock State Historic Landmark, southwest of Casper, is a huge granite boulder where more than five thousand emigrants along the Oregon Trail carved their names.

Oregon Trail Ruts National Historic Landmark, south of Guernsey, is a long stretch of the Oregon Trail where thousands of wagon wheels gradually wore deep ruts in the soft sandstone above the North Platte River.

South Pass City is the site of a gold-mining boomtown that sprang up in 1867 and folded by 1872. More than twenty historic buildings are on display at the site.

Trail End Historic Center, near Sheridan, is housed in the Flemish-style mansion that was the home of governor and senator John B. Kendrick. The house, built in 1913, is surrounded by many species of native trees transplanted from all over the state.

121

Other Interesting Places to Visit:

Bighorn Canyon National Recreation Area, surrounding the Bighorn River in northern Wyoming and extending into Montana, is a scenic area of colorful, fossil-laden cliffs.

Devils Tower National Monument, northwest of Sundance, is a towering, stump-shaped cluster of volcanic rock that became the nation's first national monument in 1906.

Flaming Gorge National Recreation Area, south of Green River and extending into Utah, is a 201,000-acre (81,343-hectare) scenic wilderness of deserts, naturally sculptured rock formations, and colorfully layered canyons surrounding Flaming Gorge Lake.

Fossil Butte National Monument, west of Kemmerer, is a geological formation that contains the world's largest and most diverse deposits of fossilized fish.

Grand Teton National Park, south of Yellowstone National Park, is an area of glistening lakes, abundant wildlife, and snowcapped mountain peaks rising above Jackson Hole.

Historic Governors' Mansion, in Cheyenne, housed Wyoming's governors from 1905 to 1976.

Medicine Wheel, near Lovell, is a circle of white, flat stones, 70 ft. (21 m) in diameter, that may have been used as a calendar by prehistoric Indians.

National Elk Refuge, in Jackson Hole, is the winter home of thousands of elk.

Old Frontier Prison, in Rawlins, operated as the Wyoming State Prison from 1901 to 1981. Visitors to the prison can see the original cell blocks, dining room, gas chamber, and exercise areas.

Wind River Canyon, between Shoshoni and Thermopolis, is a scenic gorge between the Bridger and Owl Creek mountains; its layered cliffs show successive eras in Wyoming's geologic history.

Wind River Indian Reservation, in the Wind River Mountains and Basin, is home to Eastern Shoshone and Northern Arapahoe Indians and contains the burial grounds of Shoshone chief Washakie and Shoshone guide Sacajawea.

Wyoming Territorial Prison, west of Laramie, was the holding pen for some of the most notorious outlaws in the West, including Butch Cassidy. It operated from 1872 to 1902.

Yellowstone National Park, in Wyoming's northwest corner, contains the world's largest array of geysers and other thermal features; also in the park are the breathtaking canyon and falls of the Yellowstone River.

IMPORTANT DATES

c. 18,000 B.C.—Paleo-Indians begin to move into present-day Wyoming

c. 9000 B.C.—Early Hunters flourish in Wyoming

c. 7000 B.C.—People begin occupying the Mummy Cave area

A.D. 1743—French Canadians François and Louis Joseph de la Vérendrye become the first known whites to enter present-day Wyoming

1803—Most of Wyoming, as part of the Louisiana Purchase, becomes United States territory

1807—John Colter becomes the first known white person to explore the Yellowstone park region

1811—Wilson Price Hunt of the American Fur Company travels through Wyoming

1812—Robert Stuart of the Pacific Fur Company discovers South Pass, a pass through the Rocky Mountains

1822—William Henry Ashley and Andrew Henry organize the Rocky Mountain Fur Company

1824—Jedediah Smith leads a party through South Pass and into the Green River Basin

1825—At Henrys Fork of the Green River, William Henry Ashley of the Rocky Mountain Fur Company holds the first annual rendezvous for fur trappers

1829—William Sublette names Jackson Lake and Jackson Hole after fellow trapper David Jackson

1833—Captain Benjamin de Bonneville finds an oil spring in the Wind River Valley

1834—William Sublette and Robert Campbell build Wyoming's first permanent white settlement, Fort William (later renamed Fort Laramie)

1839—Thomas Farnham becomes the first of thousands of pioneers to take a route through Wyoming to Oregon

1840—The last Rocky Mountain fur trappers' rendezvous is held, on Horse Creek of the Green River

1842-43—Lieutenant John Charles Frémont, with Kit Carson as a guide, surveys Wyoming; Jim Bridger opens Fort Bridger trading post on the Blacks Fork River

1847—Brigham Young leads Mormon followers through Wyoming along the Mormon Trail to Utah

1849—California-bound gold seekers begin traveling through Wyoming on the California Trail; the U.S. Army buys Fort Laramie

1851—In a council at Fort Laramie, Indians agree not to bother travelers on the Oregon Trail

1854—In the Grattan Massacre, Lieutenant John Grattan and twenty-nine soldiers are killed in a battle with Indians east of Fort Laramie

1853—Mormons purchase Fort Bridger

1857—In the Mormon War, Mormons burn Fort Bridger and leave southwest Wyoming

1858—Fort Bridger becomes a military fort

1860—The Pony Express route runs through Wyoming

1864—John W. Bozeman establishes the Bozeman Trail through the Powder River Basin into Montana; Jim Bridger establishes the Bridger Trail from Casper across the Bighorn Basin into Montana

1865—In the Battle of Tongue River, General Patrick Connor stages a surprise attack on Cheyenne and Arapahoe villages

1866—Fort Phil Kearny and Fort Reno are established to protect travelers along the Bozeman Trail; chiefs Red Cloud and Crazy Horse ambush and kill Lieutenant Colonel William Fetterman and eighty-one soldiers

1867—The Union Pacific Railroad enters Wyoming; Cheyenne is founded, Fort Fetterman is built northwest of present-day Douglas; gold strikes lead to the founding of Atlantic City and South Pass City; in the Wagon Box Fight, timber cutters fend off Sioux and Cheyenne warriors near Fort Phil Kearny

1868—Congress establishes Wyoming Territory; in the Treaty of Fort Laramie, the Sioux agree not to attack builders of the transcontinental railroad; the Eastern Shoshone are assigned to the Wind River Indian Reservation; cattleman Nelson Story drives the first herd of Texas longhorn cattle through Wyoming to Montana

1869—The territorial legislature passes the nation's first woman suffrage bill; the Union Pacific Railroad is completed through Wyoming

1870—Esther Hobart Morris is appointed justice of the peace in South Pass city, becoming the nation's first female judge; in Laramie, Eliza Swain becomes the first woman in the nation to cast a vote in a general election

1872—Congress establishes Yellowstone National Park as the nation's first national park

1873—Ranchers form the Laramie County Stock Growers' Association

1874—Gold is discovered in the Black Hills, starting a gold rush that causes strife in the Powder River Basin

1876—At the Red Fork of the Powder River, General MacKenzie defeats Chief Dull Knife in the last major battle of Wyoming's Indian wars; the Cheyenne-to-Deadwood stagecoach line opens, leading to the gold fields near Deadwood, South Dakota

1877—Arapahoe Indians are settled in the Wind River reservation as a supposedly temporary measure

1883—Wyoming's first oil well is drilled in the Dallas Field; "Buffalo Bill" Cody begins his Wild West show

1886—The University of Wyoming is founded at Laramie

1886-87—A severe winter kills many cattle

1887—Wyoming's capitol building is completed in Cheyenne

1888—Oil drilling begins in the Casper area

1889—Oil is discovered in the Salt Creek field north of Casper

1890—Wyoming becomes the nation's forty-fourth state

1892—Cattlemen kill two suspected rustlers in what becomes known as the Johnson County War

1894—The Carey Act is passed, encouraging homesteading; Estelle Reel is voted Wyoming's superintendent of education, becoming the first woman in the nation to hold a state elective office

1897—Copper is discovered in the Sierra Madre in south-central Wyoming

1902—President Theodore Roosevelt establishes Medicine Bow National Forest; in Kemmerer, J. C. Penney opens the first of his retail stores

1901—Wyoming State Prison opens in Rawlins

1905—First annual Wyoming State Fair is held in Douglas

1906—Devils Tower becomes the nation's first national monument

1908—Teton National Forest is established

1909—In the Spring Creek Raid, the last of the great range wars, cattlemen kill three sheepherders near Ten Sleep; Pathfinder Dam on the North Platte River is completed

1910—Shoshone Dam (now Buffalo Bill Dam) is completed on the Shoshone River

1911—Bridger National Forest is established

1912—Oil is discovered in the Salt Creek Field north of Casper; oil and natural gas are discovered near Glenrock

1922—Secretary of the Interior Albert Fall illegally leases the Teapot Dome oil reserve to Harry Sinclair's oil company

1924—Nellie Tayloe Ross is elected governor of Wyoming, becoming the nation's first woman governor

1929—Congress establishes Grand Teton National Park

1935—Construction begins on the Kendrick Project, designed to bring irrigation to the North Platte Valley

1937—Shoshone Indians sue the U.S. government for the value of lands occupied by the Arapahoe on the Wind River Indian Reservation

1943—Jackson Hole National Monument is established

1947—Trona mining begins in the Green River Basin

1950—Jackson Hole National Monument is incorporated into Grand Teton National Park

1951—Wyoming's first uranium is discovered in the Powder River area

1960—F. E. Warren Air Force Base becomes the nation's first intercontinental ballistic missile base

1968—Congress establishes Flaming Gorge National Recreation Area in southwestern Wyoming and northeastern Utah

1969—Wyoming's legislature passes a stiff severance tax on mineral extraction in the state

1972—Congress establishes the John D. Rockefeller, Jr. Memorial Parkway through Grand Teton National Park; Fossil Butte National Monument is established

1973—Bridger and Teton national forests are merged to form Bridger-Teton National Forest, the state's largest national forest

1974—Jim Bridger Power Plant in Rock Springs begins operation

1982—Wyoming's coal severance tax is raised to 17.5 percent

1984—President Ronald Reagan signs the Wyoming Wilderness Act, establishing the Gros Ventre Wilderness and enlarging the Bridger Wilderness

1988—Forest fires rage through Yellowstone National Park

1990—Centennial celebrations are held across the state

IMPORTANT PEOPLE

THURMAN ARNOLD

Thurman Wesley Arnold (1891-1969), lawyer, judge; born in Laramie; professor at Yale University (1930-37); as assistant U.S. attorney general (1938-43), prosecuted some 230 antitrust cases; judge for U.S. Court of Appeals for Washington, D.C. (1943-45); his books include *The Folklore of Capitalism* (1937)

Benjamin Louis Eulalie de Bonneville (1796-1878), army officer, explorer; while leading an expedition through Wyoming in the 1830s, crossed through the Rockies at South Pass, explored the Green River area, and found oil in the Wind River Basin; was the subject of Washington Irving's *Adventures of Captain Bonneville*

JIM BRIDGER

James (Jim) Bridger (1804-1881), pioneer, trapper, scout; explored Wyoming's Rocky Mountain regions as a partner in the Rocky Mountain Fur Company; in 1824, became the first white man to visit Utah's Great Salt Lake; in 1842, built Fort Bridger in southwest Wyoming, which served as a supply post for travelers along various westbound trails; in 1864, established the Bridger Trail, over which he led travelers to the Montana gold fields

LIZ BYRD

ROBERT CAREY

DICK CHENEY

PEGGY CURRY

Maxwell Struthers Burt (1882-1954), novelist; became a Wyoming rancher in 1908; his many books include *In the High Hills, Diary of a Dude Wrangler,* and *Powder River*

Harriet Elizabeth (Liz) Byrd (1926-   ), born in Cheyenne; politician; Wyoming state representative (1981-90); Wyoming state senator (1991-   ); worked to establish the Dr. Martin Luther King, Jr., Holiday as a state holiday

Joseph M. Carey (1845-1924), rancher, judge, politician; served as a Wyoming territorial judge; in 1885, organized the Wyoming Development Company to bring water to the Wheatland area; as a U.S. senator from Wyoming (1890-95), introduced the Wyoming statehood bill and wrote the 1894 Carey Act, which enabled more homesteaders to settle in Wyoming; governor of Wyoming (1911-15)

Robert D. Carey (1878-1937), politician; son of Joseph M. Carey; U.S. senator from Wyoming (1931-36)

Richard (Dick) Cheney (1941-   ), politician; was educated at the University of Wyoming; deputy assistant to the U.S. president (1974-75); assistant to the president (1975-77); U.S. representative from Wyoming (1979-89); U.S. secretary of defense (1989-   )

John Ford Clymer (1907-1987), artist, illustrator; resident of Teton Village; specialized in western subjects; painted more than eighty covers for the *Saturday Evening Post* (1942-62); received the National Academy of Western Artists' gold medal in 1974; his paintings hang in permanent collections in Wyoming and throughout the West

William Frederick "Buffalo Bill" Cody (1846-1917), frontiersman, scout, showman; rode for the Pony Express (1860); acquired the nickname "Buffalo Bill" while hunting buffalo to feed railroad crews; while working as a scout for the army, helped fight Indians in Colorado and Wyoming (1876); performed as an actor (1872-83); organized a traveling show called Buffalo Bill's Wild West, which gained international fame; founded the town of Cody

John Colter (1775?-1813), explorer; took part in the Lewis and Clark Expedition (1804-06); while on Manuel Lisa's 1807 trapping expedition, became the first white person to travel through the Yellowstone park region; an area of thermal activity along the Shoshone River west of Cody was nicknamed Colter's Hell because of his descriptions

Peggy Simpson Curry (1911-   ), novelist; was born in Scotland and came to the U.S. as a child; graduated from the University of Wyoming and later moved to Casper; her books include *Fire in the Water, Red Wind of Wyoming, So Far from Spring,* and *The Oil Patch*

John Charles Frémont (1813-1890), soldier, explorer, politician; led a surveying expedition through central Wyoming in 1842 and southern Wyoming in 1843

Curtis (Curt) Gowdy (1919-   ), sportscaster; born in Green River; distinguished himself as a major network television sportscaster for both baseball and football games; named to the Sports Broadcasters Hall of Fame (1981), the Baseball Hall of Fame (1984), and the American Sportscasters Hall of Fame (1985); Curt Gowdy State Park, between Cheyenne and Laramie, is named for him

CURT GOWDY

Ferdinand Vandeveer Hayden (1829-1887), geologist; as part of the U.S. Geological Survey, explored the Rocky Mountains (1869-79); on expeditions into the Yellowstone, Grand Teton, and Jackson Hole areas in 1871, 1872, 1877, and 1878, named several of the region's geological features; urged that Yellowstone become a national park

Grace Raymond Hebard (1861-1936), historian, librarian, educator; came to Laramie from Iowa as a young woman and became a librarian and professor of history at the University of Wyoming; conducted extensive research and wrote numerous books on Wyoming and western history; campaigned for woman suffrage

Edward Herschler (1918-1990), lawyer, politician; only person in Wyoming history to serve three terms as governor (1975-87)

FERDINAND HAYDEN

David E. Jackson (1790?-1837), trapper, mountain man; partner with Jedediah Smith, James Bridger, and William Sublette in the Rocky Mountain Fur Company (1829-34); Sublette named Jackson Hole and Jackson Lake after him in 1829

Harry Andrew Jackson (1924-   ), sculptor; resident of Cody; his many one-person shows have included an exhibit at the Smithsonian Institution; his works are in the permanent collections of major museums throughout the U.S.; was commissioned to make the large, bronze Sacajawea monument at the Plains Indian Museum

ED HERSCHLER

John B. Kendrick (1857-1933), rancher, politician; governor of Wyoming (1915-17); Wyoming's first Democratic U.S. senator (1917-33); worked long and hard for approval of the Kendrick Project for the North Platte Valley; Trail End, his palatial home near Sheridan, is a state historic site

Taft Alfred (T.A.) Larson (1910-   ); educator, historian; resident of Laramie; foremost authority on Wyoming history; author of four books on Wyoming history; taught at the University of Wyoming for thirty-nine years

Chris LeDoux (1949-   ), cowboy, singer, rodeo champion; moved to Cheyenne as a teenager; won the world championship bareback riding title at the National Rodeo Finals in Oklahoma City (1976); wrote and recorded songs about rodeo life

HARRY JACKSON

ESTHER MORRIS

BILL NYE

JOSEPH O'MAHONEY

JOHN WESLEY POWELL

Caroline Lockhart (1875-1962), journalist, novelist; moved to Cody in 1904; her seven novels, all based on various Cody characters, brought her national attention as a western writer; they include *Me-Smith* and *The Old West and the New*

Frank W. Mondell (1860-1939), prospector, politician; in the late 1880s, discovered coal in northeastern Wyoming; mayor of Newcastle (1890-95); as a U.S. representative from Wyoming (1895-97, 1899-1923), was chairman of the House Committee on Public Lands; majority leader of the House of Representatives (1919-23)

Thomas Moran (1837-1926), English-born artist; traveling in northwest Wyoming with the Hayden survey party in the 1870s, he made sketches of the scenery and later developed them into paintings in a panoramic study called *The Grand Canyon of the Yellowstone*; many of his paintings were the first ever made of those subjects; Mount Moran, in the Teton range, is named for him

Esther Hobart Morris (1814-1902), judge; appointed justice of the peace for South Pass City (1870), becoming the nation's first female judge

Edgar Wilson (Bill) Nye (1850-1896), humorist, journalist; moved to Wyoming in 1876, served in the territorial legislature, and was Laramie's postmaster and justice of the peace; editor (1881-83) of Laramie's Republican party newspaper, *Boomerang*, named for Nye's mule; widely known for his humorous writings, he was hired by the *New York World* in 1883 and later collaborated with James Whitcomb Riley

Ted Olson (1899-   ), poet; began his writing career as a journalist in Laramie

Joseph Christopher O'Mahoney (1884-1962), journalist, lawyer, politician; was appointed first assistant postmaster general of the U.S. in 1933 and resigned to become a U.S. senator from Wyoming (1934-60); opposed President Franklin D. Roosevelt's "Supreme Court-packing" bill in 1937

Paul Jackson Pollock (1912-1956), artist; born in Cody; one of the leading painters in the abstract expressionist style, he is known for his technique of dripping or pouring paint onto his canvases

John Wesley Powell (1834-1902), army officer, geologist, explorer; in 1869, led an expedition down the Green River, eventually reaching the Colorado River and becoming the first to explore Arizona's Grand Canyon by boat; led a second expedition in 1871; became director of the United States Geological Survey (1881) and served as first director of the Smithsonian Institution's Bureau of Ethnology (1879-1902)

John Davison Rockefeller, Jr. (1874-1960), industrialist, philanthropist; worked with the oil empire established by his father; contributed 52 sq. mi. (135 km²) of his own grazing land to Jackson Hole National Monument, which later become part of Grand Teton National Park; the memorial parkway through Grand Teton is named for him

Nellie Tayloe Ross (1876-1977), politician; after her husband, Wyoming governor William Bradford Ross, died in office, she was elected governor to complete his term (1925-27), becoming the nation's first female governor; director of the U.S. Mint (1933-53)

NELLIE TAYLOE ROSS

Robert Isaiah Russin (1914-   ), sculptor; professor of art at the University of Wyoming (1947-86); artist-in-residence at the university (1976-86); institutions from all over the world have commissioned his sculptures of bronze, marble, or steel; in Wyoming, his work appears in Cheyenne, Laramie, Casper, and other cities; his sculpture *The Family* stands on the University of Wyoming campus

Sacajawea (1787?-1884), Shoshone Indian who served as a guide for the Lewis and Clark Expedition (1804-05); kidnapped from the Shoshone by the Hidatsa, she was the wife of trapper Touissant Charbonneau when both joined Lewis and Clark; later married a Comanche Indian in Oklahoma; returned to live among the Shoshone in the 1840s; she is said to be buried west of Fort Washakie

ALAN SIMPSON

Alan Kooi Simpson (1931-   ), politician; born in Cody; son of Milward Simpson; as a state representative (1964-77), fought for environmental planning; U.S. senator from Wyoming (1978-   )

Milward Lee Simpson (1897-   ), lawyer, politician; governor of Wyoming (1955-59); U.S. senator from Wyoming (1963-69)

Gerald (Gerry) Spence (1929-   ), born in Laramie; lawyer, writer; one of the nation's top trial lawyers; has won some of the biggest court judgments in history, including the 1976 Karen Silkwood case

MILWARD SIMPSON

William Lewis Sublette (1799?-1845), mountain man, trapper, explorer; came to the Rocky Mountains with William Ashley in 1823; partner in the Rocky Mountain Fur Company (1829-34); brought the first wagons into the Rocky Mountains on his 1829 trip from St. Louis, Missouri, to the Wind River region; in 1829, named Jackson Hole after his partner David Jackson; with Robert Campbell, built Fort Laramie in 1834; part of the Oregon Trail was named Sublette's Cutoff after him

Willis Van Devanter (1859-1941), lawyer, judge; opened a law practice in Cheyenne (1884); chief justice of Wyoming Territory (1888-90), U.S. circuit judge for the eighth circuit (1903-10); associate justice of the U.S. Supreme Court (1910-37)

WILLIS VAN DEVANTER

WASHAKIE

OWEN WISTER

Francis E. Warren (1844-1929), politician; first governor of the state of Wyoming (1890); U.S. senator from Wyoming (1890-1929); Cheyenne's Francis E. Warren Air Force Base is named for him

Washakie (1798?-1900), Shoshone Indian leader; spent much of his life in Wyoming; became chief of the Eastern Shoshone in the 1840s; fought for land and protection for his people and helped the army in battles against the Sioux; signed the 1868 Treaty of Fort Bridger, allowing railroads to be built through Shoshone lands; lived on the Wind River Indian Reservation from 1868 until his death; was buried in the reservation's old military cemetery with military honors, the first ever bestowed on an Indian chief

James Gaius Watt (1938-   ), politician; born in Lusk; from 1962, held various offices in the U.S. Department of the Interior; U.S. secretary of the interior (1981-83); after resigning in 1983, practiced law in Washington, D.C., and Jackson Hole

Owen Wister (1860-1938), novelist; his experiences in Wyoming, and especially around Medicine Bow, provided much of the material for his novel *The Virginian*; other works include *Red Men and White*, and *The Pentecost of Calamity*

GOVERNORS

Francis E. Warren	1890	Lester C. Hunt	1943-1949
Amos W. Barber	1890-1893	Arthur Griswold Crane	1949-1951
John E. Osborne	1893-1895	Frank A. Barrett	1951-1953
William A. Richards	1895-1899	C. J. Rogers	1953-1955
DeForest Richards	1899-1903	Milward L. Simpson	1955-1959
Fenimore Chatterton	1903-1905	J. J. Hickey	1959-1961
Bryant B. Brooks	1905-1911	Jack R. Gage	1961-1963
Joseph M. Carey	1911-1915	Clifford P. Hansen	1963-1967
John B. Kendrick	1915-1917	Stanley K. Hathaway	1967-1975
Frank L. Houx	1917-1919	Edward J. Herschler	1975-1987
Robert D. Carey	1919-1923	Mike Sullivan	1987-
William B. Ross	1923-1924		
Frank E. Lucas	1924-1925		
Nellie Tayloe Ross	1925-1927		
Frank C. Emerson	1827-1931		
Alonzo M. Clark	1931-1933		
Leslie A. Miller	1933-1939		
Nels H. Smith	1939-1943		

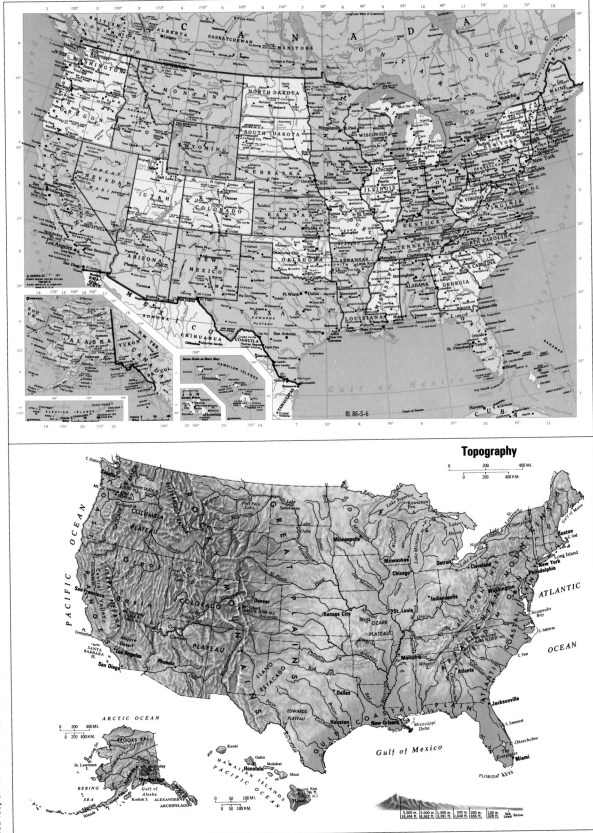

Topography

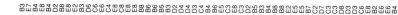

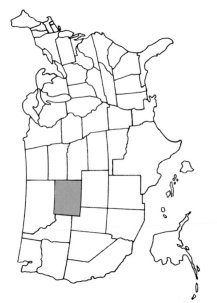

MAP KEY

Absaroka Range	B3
Acme	B6
Aton	B8
Aladdin	B8
Albany	E6
Albin	E8
Alcova	D6
Alpine	D2
Alta	C1
Alva	B8
Antelope Butte	B7
Antelope Creek	C7
Arapahoe	D4
Arminto	C5
Arter, Mount	C4
Arvada	B6
Atlantic City	D4
Atlantic Peak	D4
Auburn	D1
Badwater River	C5
Baggs	E5
Bald Mountain	B5
Basin	B6
Bear Creek	E8
Bear Lodge Mountains	B8
Bear River	E1, E2
Beartooth Mountains	A3
Beartooth Pass	B3
Beaver Creek	C8
Beaver Creek	D2
Bedford	D2
Belle Fourche River	B7
Beulah	B8
Bill	C7
Big Horn	B5
Big Piney	D2
Big Sandy Reservoir	D3
Big Sandy River	D3
Bighorn Canyon Recreation Area	A4
Bighorn Lake	B5
Bighorn Mountains	B5
Bighorn River	C4
Bill	C7
Bitter Creek	E4
Black Butte	E4
Black Hills	B5
Black Mountain	D7
Blackhall Mountain	D7
Blacks Fork	E3
Bondurant	D2
Bonneville	C4
Bosler	E6
Boulder	D3
Bridger Mountains	C4
Bridger Peak	E5
Buffalo	B6
Buffalo Bill Reservoir	B3
Buford	E7
Burlington	B4
Burns	E8
Byron	B4
Calpet	D2
Carlile	B8
Carpenter	E8
Carter	E2
Carter Mountain	B3
Casper	C6
Casper Creek	D6
Centennial	E6
Chatham	C4
Cheyenne	E8
Cheyenne River	B6
Chugwater	D4
Chugwater Creek	D7
Clay	D3
Clear Creek	C5
Clearmont	B6
Cloud Peak	B5
Cody	B4
Cokeville	E2
Continental Divide	E8
Continental Peak	E1, E2
Cora	D2
Cottonwood Creek	A3
Cowley	B4
Crazy Woman Creek	B6
Creston	E5
Crosby, Mount	D2
Crow Creek	B7
Crowheart	C4
Daniel	D2
Dayton	B5
Dead Indian Peak	B3
Deaver	B4
Devils Tower National Monument	B8
Diamondville	E2
Divide Peak	E5
Dixon	E5
Donkey Creek	B7
Doubletop Peak	D3
Douglas	D7
Downs Mountain	C3
Dubois	C3
Dwyer	D7
East River	E3
Eden	E3
Edgerton	C6
Egbert	E8
Electric Peak	B2
Elk Mountain	E5
Elk Mountain	C4
Emblem	B6
Encampment	E6
Esterbrook	D7
Ethete	D4
Etna	D2
Evanston	E2
Evansville	C6
Fairview	D2
Falls River	B2
Farson	D3
Ferris Mountains	D5
Fivemile Creek	C4
Flaming Gorge Recreation Area	E3
Flaming Gorge Reservoir	E3
Fontenelle	E2
Fontenelle Reservoir	D2
Fort Bridger	E2
Fort Laramie	D8
Fort Laramie National Historic Site	D8
Fort Steele	E5
Fort Washakie	C4
Fortress Mountain	B3
Fossil Butte National Monument	E2
Four Corners	B8
Foxpark	E6
Francs Peak	C3
Fremont Lake	D3
Fremont Peak	D3
Frontier	E2
Gallatin Range	A2
Gannett Peak	C3
Garland	B4
Garrett	D7
Gas Hills	D5
Gillette	B7
Glendo	D7
Glendo Reservoir	D7
Glenrock	C6
Gooseberry Creek	C4
Grand Teton, mountain	C2
Grand Teton National Park	C2
Granger	E3
Granite Canyon	E8
Granite Mountains	D5
Granite Pass	B5
Granite Peak	D4
Grass Creek	C4
Great Divide, basin	E4
Green Mountains	D5
Green River	E3
Greybull	B4
Greybull River	B4
Greys River	D2
Gros Ventre Range	C2
Gros Ventre River	C2
Grover	D2
Guernsey	D8
Hamilton Dome	C4
Hams Fork	D2
Hanna	E6
Harriman	E8
Hartville	D8
Hawk Springs	E8
Hazelton Peak	B6
Heart Lake	C2
Henrys Fork	E3
Hiland	C5
Hillsdale	E8
Hoback River	D2
Holmes, Mount	B2
Horse Creek	E8
Hudson	D4
Hulett	B8
Huntley	D8
Hunt Mountain	B5
Hyattville	B5
Indian Peak	C3
Iron Mountain	E7
Jackson	C2
Jackson Lake	C2
James Town	E5
Jay Em	D8
Jeffrey City	D5
Jelm	E6
John D. Rockefeller, Jr. Memorial Parkway	C2
Kaycee	C6
Keeline	D8
Kelly	C2
Kemmerer	E2
Kennaday Peak	E6
Keyhole Reservoir	B8
Kinnear	C4
Kirby	C4
La Barge	D2
La Barge Creek	D2
Lagrange	E8
Lamont	D5
Lance Creek	C8
Lander	D4
Laramie	E7
Laramie Mountains	D7
Laramie Peak	D7
Laramie River	E6
Leiter	B6
Lewis Lake	C2
Lewis River	C2
Lightning Creek	C8
Linch	C6
Lingle	D8
Little Bighorn River	B5
Little Goose Creek	B5
Little Laramie River	E6
Little Missouri River	B8
Little Mountain	C4
Little Powder River	B7
Little Sandy Creek	D3
Little Snake River	E5
Lizard Head Peak	D3
Lodgepole Creek	E6
Lonetree	E3
Lost Cabin	C5
Lost Springs	D7
Lovell	B4
Lusk	C8
Lyman	E2
Lysite	C5
Manderson	B5
Manville	C8
Marbleton	D2
Mather Peaks	B5
McDougal, Mount	D2
McFadden	E6
McKinnon	E3
Medicine Bow	E6
Medicine Bow Mountains	E6
Medicine Bow Peak	E6
Medicine Bow River	E6
Meeteetse	B4
Meriden	E8
Midwest	C6
Mills	C6
Missouri Buttes	B8
Moorcroft	B7
Moose	C2
Moran	C2
Mountain View	E2
Muddy Creek	E5
Muddy Gap	D5
Natrona	C5
Needle Mountain	B3
Newcastle	C8
Niobrara River	D8
Node	D8
North Laramie River	D7
North Platte River	E6
Nowood River	B5
Orchard Valley	E8
Osage	C8
Oshoto	B8
Otto	B4
Owl Creek	C4
Owl Creek Mountains	C4
Oyster Ridge	E2
Pacific Creek	C3
Pahaska	B3
Paradise Valley	D6
Park Range	E5
Parkman	B5
Pathfinder Reservoir	D6
Pavillion	C4
Pilot Peak	B3
Pine Bluffs	E8
Pinedale	D3
Pinnacle Buttes	C3
Pisgah, Mount	E3
Point of Rocks	E4
Poison River	D5
Powder River	C6
Powder River Pass	B5
Powell	B4
Prater Mountain	C3
Pumpkin Buttes	C7
Pyramid Peak	C2
Ragged Top Mountain	D5
Ralston	B4
Ramshorn Peak	C3
Ranchester	B5
Rattlesnake Hills	D5
Rawhide Creek	D8
Rawlins	E5
Recluse	B7
Red Buttes Village	D6
Red Desert	E4
Reliance	E4
Riverside	E7
Riverton	D7(?)
Roberts Mountain	E7
Robertson	E2
Rock Creek	B6
Rock River	B2
Rock Springs	E4
Rozet	B7
Ryan Park	E6
Saddlestring	B6
Salt Creek	C6
Salt River Range	D2
Salt Wells Creek	E4
Sand Creek	B8
Saratoga	E5
Savery	E5
Seminoe Dam	D5
Seminoe Mountains	E6(?)
Seminoe Reservoir	D5
Shawnee	D7
Sheep Mountain	E6
Shell	B5
Shell Creek	B5
Sheridan	B5
Sheridan, Mount	C2
Shirley Basin	D6
Shoshone Lake	C2
Shoshone River	B4
Shoshoni	C4
Sinclair	E5
Smoot	D2
Snake River	D2
Snake River Range	C2
South Pass	D3
South Pass City	D4
South Superior	E4
South Torrington	D8
Squaw Hill	B8
Story	B5
Sundance	B8
Sunlight Creek	B3
Sunrise	D8
Superior	E4
Sweetwater River	D4
Sweetwater Station	D4
Sylvan Pass	C2
Ten Sleep	C5
Teton Pass	C2
Teton Range	C2
Teton Village	C2
Thayne	D2
Thermopolis	C4
Tie Siding	E7
Tongue River	B5
Torrington	D8
Trout Peak	B3
Tump Range	D2
Twin Mountains	E5
Upton	C8
Van Tassell	C8
Veteran	D8
Walcott	E5
Wamsutter	E4
Wapiti	B3
Wapiti Ridge	B3
Warren Peaks	B8
Washakie Needles, mountain	C3
Washburn, Mount	B2
West Laramie	E7
Weston	B7
Wheatland	D7
Wiggins Peak	C3
Willow Creek	C4
Wind River	C4
Wind River Indian Reservation	C4
Wind River Peak	D3
Wind River Range	C3
Wolf	B5
Wood River	B4
Worland	B5
Wyarno	B6
Wyodak	B7
Wyoming Peak	D2
Wyoming Range	D2
Yellowstone Lake	C2
Yellowstone National Park	B3
Yellowstone River	B2
Yoder	D5(?)

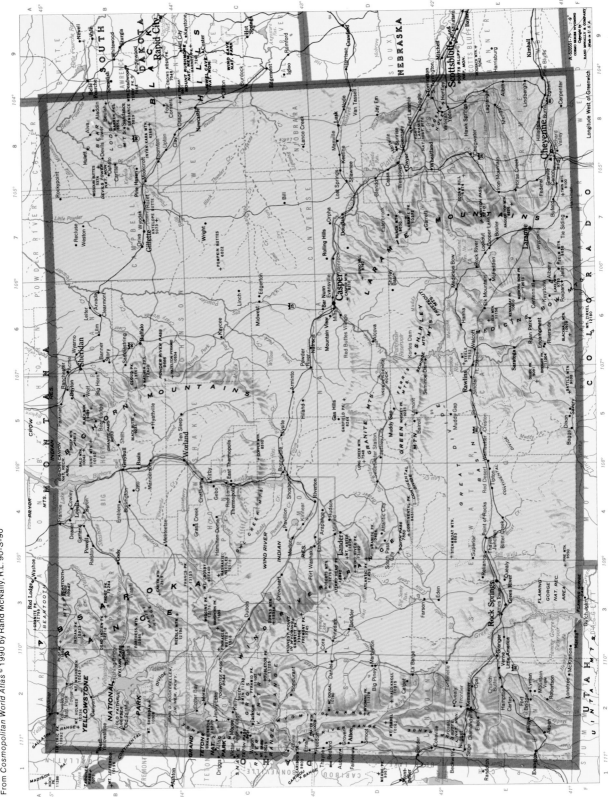

From *Cosmopolitan World Atlas* © 1990 by Rand McNally, R.L. 90-S-90

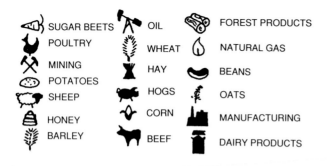

SUGAR BEETS	OIL	FOREST PRODUCTS
POULTRY	WHEAT	NATURAL GAS
MINING	HAY	BEANS
POTATOES	HOGS	OATS
SHEEP	CORN	MANUFACTURING
HONEY	BEEF	DAIRY PRODUCTS
BARLEY		

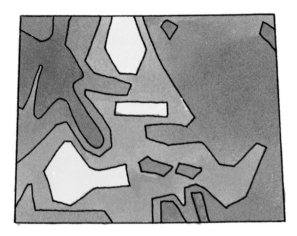

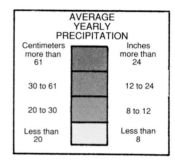

AVERAGE YEARLY PRECIPITATION

Centimeters		Inches
more than 61		more than 24
30 to 61		12 to 24
20 to 30		8 to 12
Less than 20		Less than 8

MAJOR HIGHWAYS

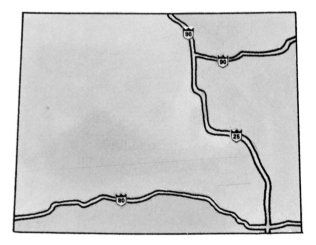

POPULATION DENSITY

Number of persons per square kilometer		Number of persons per square mile
more than 4		more than 10
2 to 4		5 to 10
1 to 2		2 to 5
Less than 1		Less than 2

TOPOGRAPHY

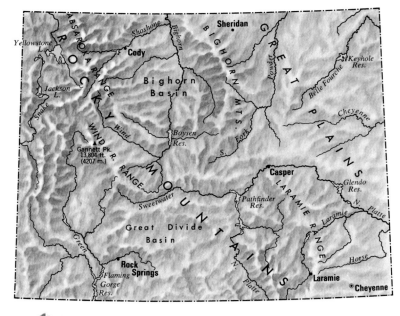

5,000 m.	2,000 m.	1,000 m.	500 m.	200 m.	100 m.	Sea	Below
16,404 ft.	6,562 ft.	3,281 ft.	1,640 ft.	656 ft.	328 ft.	Level	

Courtesy of Hammond, Incorporated
Maplewood, New Jersey

COUNTIES

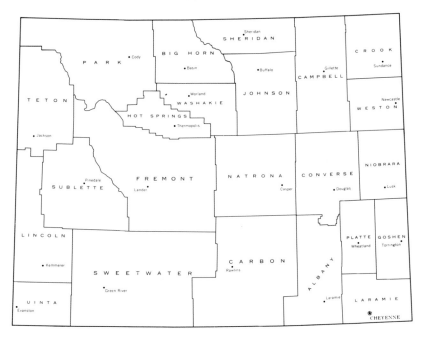

Examples
of nature's
rebirth
after the
devastating
Yellowstone
fires of 1988

INDEX

Page numbers that appear in boldface type indicate illustrations

A cattle drive in the Bighorn Mountains

Picture Identifications
Front cover: The Tetons
Pages 2-3: A hay field near Castle Rock in the Absaroka Mountains
Page 6: A cowboy riding saddle bronc during Cheyenne's Frontier Days
Pages 8-9: Grand Teton and Mount Owen
Pages 22-23: Montage of Wyoming residents
Page 28: Native Americans in traditional dress during a festival in Ethete
Page 40: Nineteenth-century westward-bound emigrants
Page 52: Buffalo Bill Cody (on horse at left) in front of the Irma Hotel in Cody
Page 64: The state capitol building in Cheyenne
Pages 76-77: A chromolithograph by nineteenth-century artist Thomas Moran of Great Blue Spring in Yellowstone National Park
Pages 88-89: Porcelain Basin, Norris Geyser Basin, Yellowstone National Park
Page 108: Montage of state symbols, including the state flag, state tree (plains cottonwood), state flower (Indian paintbrush), state mammal (bison), and state bird (meadowlark)
Back cover: Mammoth Springs, Yellowstone National Park

Picture Acknowledgments

Front cover, © Bob & Suzanne Clemenz/**Bob Clemenz Photography**; 2-3, © Tom Dietrich; 4, © Woodall & Mckoy/JH Ski Corp./**Wyoming Division of Tourism** 5, © Stan Osolinski/**Dembinsky Photo Assoc.**; 6, © Tom Dietrich; 8-9, © E. Cooper/**H. Armstrong Roberts**; 11, © **Tom Dietrich**; 12 (left), © M. Schneiders/**H. Armstrong Roberts**; 13 (left), © Bob & Suzanne Clemenz/**Bob Clemenz Photography**; 13 (right), © **Bob Clemenz Photography**; 14, © Tom Dietrich; 15, © **Bob Clemenz Photography**; 17, © Karl Fliehler/**Tony Stone Worldwide/Chicago Ltd.**; 18 (left), © Everett C. Johnson/**Marilyn Gartman Agency**; 18 (right), © Everett C. Johnson/**Marilyn Gartman Agency**; 18 (right), © Earl L. Kubis/**R/C Photo Agency**; 20, © David L. Brown/**Journalism Services**; 22 (top left), © **Tom Dietrich**; 22 (bottom left), © **Eric Futran**; 22 (bottom right), © **Larsh K. Bristol**; 22 (top right), 23 (top left), © **John Running**; 23 (top right), © L. L. T. Rhodes/**Tony Stone Worldwide/Chicago Ltd.**; 23 (bottom left), © Tom Dietrich; 23 (bottom right), © Bob Winsett/**Tom Stack & Associates**; 26, © Jim Pickerell/**Tony Stone Worldwide/Chicago Ltd.**; 28, © **John Running**; 31, **Courtesy Amon Carter Museum, Fort Worth, Texas**; 34 (left), **Denver Public Library, Western History Department**; 34 (right), **The Kansas State Historical Society, Topeka, Kansas**; 37, **Denver Public Library, Western History Department**; 38, **Joslyn Art Museum, Omaha, Nebraska**; 40, **Denver Public Library, Western History Department**; 42, **American Heritage Center, University of Wyoming**; 47, **Wyoming State Museum**; 48 (left), **Historical Pictures Service, Inc., Chicago**; 48 (right), 51, **Denver Public Library, Western History Department**; 52, **Wyoming State Museum**; 55 (left), **Jackson Hole Museum, Teton County Historical Society, Inc., Teton County Historical Center**; 55 (right), 56, **Wyoming State Museum**; 59, **The Bettmann Archive**; 60, © W. Perry Conway/**Tom Stack & Associates**; 63, © Stan Osolinski/**Dembinsky Photo Assoc.**; 64, 67 (two photos), 68, 71, © **Tom Dietrich**; 72, © **Bob Clemenz Photography**; 73, © J. C. Allen & Son, Inc./**Root Resources**; 75, © **Joan Dunlop**; 76-77, **Courtesy Buffalo Bill Historical Center, Cody, WY**; 79, **Buffalo Bill Historical Center, Cody, WY, Gift of the Coe Foundation**; 80, **Buffalo Bill Historical Center, Cody, WY, Gift of Fred and Sara Machetanz**; 81 (two photos), © **John Running**; 83, © Sharon Gerig/**Tom Stack & Associates**; 84, © **Tom Dietrich**; 87 (left), © **Larsh K. Bristol**; 87 (right), © **John Running**; 88-89, © Stan Osolinski/**Dembinsky Photo Assoc.**; 91, 92, © Tom Dietrich; 95, © **Bob Clemenz Photography**; 95 (map), **Len Meents**; 96 (two photos), © **Tom Dietrich**; 99, © E. Cooper/**H. Armstrong Roberts**; 100, 102, © **Tom Dietrich**; 102 (map), **Len Meents**; 104 (top left), © M. Schneiders/**H. Armstrong Roberts**; 104 (bottom left), © D. Carriere/**H. Armstrong Roberts**; 104 (right), 105, © Bob & Suzanne Clemenz/**Bob Clemenz Photography**; 107, © **Tom Dietrich**; 108 (tree), © **John Running**; 108 (flag), **Courtesy Flag Research Center, Winchester, MA 01890**; 108 (bird), © Anthony Mercieca/**Root Resources**; 108 (bison), © Alan G. Nelson/**Root Resources**; 108 (flower), © **Bob & Ira Spring**; 112, © Bob & Suzanne Clemenz/**Bob Clemenz Photography**; 119, **SuperStock**; 127 (Arnold), **AP/Wide World**; 127 (Bridger), **North Wind**; 128 (Byrd), **Courtesy Liz Byrd**; 128 (Curry), *Casper-Star Tribune*; 128 (Carey, Cheney), 129 (Gowdy, Herschler, Jackson), **AP/Wide World**; 129 (Hayden), **American Heritage Center, University of Wyoming**; 130 (Nye, Powell), **North Wind**; 130 (Morris, O'Mahoney), 131 (Ross, A. Simpson, M. Simpson), **AP/Wide World**; 131 (Van Devanter), **Historical Pictures Service, Inc., Chicago**; 132 (Washakie), **Wyoming State Museum**; 132 (Wister), **AP/Wide World**; 136 (maps), **Len Meents**; 138 (two photos), © Stan Osolinski/**Dembinsky Photo Assoc.**; 141, © Phil Degginger/**Tony Stone Worldwide/Chicago, Ltd.**; back cover, © **Kirkendall/Spring**

About the Author

Ann Heinrichs is a free-lance writer and editor living in Chicago. She has worked for such educational publishers as Encyclopaedia Britannica, World Book Encyclopedia, and Science Research Associates. She is the author of a number of books, including several in the *America the Beautiful* series. Entranced by the wide-open spaces of the West, she heads out that way whenever she can.